Complying with Solicitors' Accounts Rules:
A Practical Guide

By

The Law Society Monitoring Unit

Contributors

Steve Barrow
Bob Butler
David Gibbens
Julie Hall
Chris Norton
Amanda Reade
Lisa Robotham
Fiona Smith

THE LAW SOCIETY

113 Chancery Lane
London WC2A 1PL

All rights reserved. No part of this publication may be
reproduced in any material form, whether by photocopying,
scanning, downloading onto computer or otherwise without
the written permission of the Law Society except in accordance
with the provisions of the Copyright, Designs and Patents Act 1988.
Applications should be addressed in the first instance, in writing,
to the Publications and Multimedia Department of the Law Society.
Any unauthorised or restricted act in relation to this publication
may result in civil proceedings and/or criminal prosecution.

© The Law Society 1996

ISBN 1 85328 411 4

Published by

THE LAW SOCIETY

113 Chancery Lane
London WC2A 1PL

Typeset and printed by
Multiplex medway ltd, Walderslade, Kent

Contents

	Page
Preface	vii
Introduction	ix

1. Setting Up and Using the Client Account ... 1
What is 'client's money'? ... 1
What is a 'client account'? ... 3
Signatories to the client account ... 4
Paid cheques ... 4
Separate designated accounts ... 4
Checking statements ... 5
Controlled trust accounts ... 5
Interest ... 6
Funds held jointly with third parties ... 7
Enduring powers of attorney and Court of Protection ... 7

2. The Books of Account ... 9
What are the basic requirements? ... 9
Cash books ... 9
Ledgers ... 10
Basic systems ... 10
Carbon systems ... 10
Computer systems ... 10
Deposit accounts ... 10
Inter-client transfers ... 13
Controlled trusts ... 13
Reconciliation ... 15
What other records are required? ... 15
Solicitors' Investment Business Rules ... 16
Any other points to note? ... 16

CONTENTS

3. General Accounting Systems — 17
   Money received — 17
      Post received — 17
      Receipt of client account cheques — 17
      Receipt of cash — 18
      Client account banking — 19
   Money paid out — 19
      Cleared funds — 19
      Client account cheques — 20
      Withdrawal of cash — 21
      Telegraphic transfers — 22
      Client-to-office transfers — 23
      Client-to-client transfers — 24
   Treatment of costs — 25
      Raising and delivering bills — 25
      Recording and posting of bills delivered — 25
      Receipt of costs — 26
      Costs received from the Legal Aid Board — 27
   Client account reconciliations — 28
      Requirements under Rule 11(5) — 28
      Clients' bank reconciliation statement — 29
      Clients' cash book reconciliation — 32
      Clients' matter balances — 33
      Reconciliation summary — 34
      Reconciliation of separate designated accounts — 34
      Additional points — 35
   Accounting for deposit interest — 35
      Requirements of Rule 20 — 35
      Calculating interest due on money held in general client account — 36
      Tax consequences — 37
      Controlled trusts — 37
      Compliance system — 38
   Accounting for commission received — 38
      Requirements of Solicitors' Practice Rule 10 — 38
      Accounting treatment of commission — 39
   Clients' files — 40
      File closure and archiving procedure — 40
      File retrieval system — 40

CONTENTS

4. Ensuring Compliance with the Rules   42
     The principals of the firm   42
         Responsibility   42
         Supervision   43
     The book-keeper   45
     The reporting accountant   46
     Fee earners and staff   47
     Training and development   47
         Changes to the Solicitors' Accounts Rules   47
         Changes within the firm   48
         Changes in book-keeping staff   49
         Changes in the book-keeping system used   49
     Internal security and controls   50
         Responsibility   50
         Receipt of money   51
         Withdrawal of money   51
         Safe keeping of other accounting material   53
         Organisation of the Accounts Department   54
         Fraud prevention   54

APPENDICES
     A   Solicitors' Accounts Rules 1991   57
     B   Solicitors' Accounts (Legal Aid Temporary Provision) Rule 1992   74
     C   Accountant's Report Rules 1991   75
     D   Guidance on the requirements under Rule 8(2) of the Solicitors' Accounts Rules 1991   87
     E   Guidance on deposit interest – Solicitors' Accounts Rules 1991, Part III   88
     F   Guidance on commissions   94
     G   Guidance on ownership, storage and destruction of documents   100
     H   'Blue Card' warning on money laundering – practice information   106
     I   'Green Card' warning on property fraud – practice information   110
     J   Warning issued by the Law Society regarding 'scams'   113

Preface

Since the commencement of accounts monitoring in 1993, it has become apparent that there is a need for a reference work that deals with the practical aspects of complying with the Solicitors' Accounts Rules and associated controls. This guide is aimed at filling that niche. Drawing on our experience of monitoring the accounts of a wide variety of firms, we have written it with both solicitors (sole practitioners and partners) and book-keeping staff in mind.

Apart from the avoidance of possible disciplinary action in respect of breaches of the Solicitors' Accounts Rules, it is our belief that the implementation of systems and procedures, with a view to securing full compliance with the Rules, in itself results in corresponding benefits to the firm in terms of the smooth operation of the accounts and the prompt identification and correction of any problems that may arise, thereby obviating the need for potentially costly and time-consuming retrospective action. However, in addition to addressing the compliance issues, we have also endeavoured to suggest working practices that will help the firm's accounting function to operate more efficiently and effectively.

In writing this guide, we have consulted a number of people, and would like to thank the following for their valuable contributions:

    Peter Camp, Educational and Professional Services

    Barry Hilton, The Institute of Legal Cashiers and Administrators

    Paul Venton, Chairman of Standards and Guidance Committee

    Peter Verdin, Member of Standards and Guidance Committee

    The Law Society's Professional Ethics Division

    The Law Society's Practice Advice Service

    The Investigation Accountants Department at the Solicitors Complaints Bureau

Monitoring Unit
July 1996

Introduction

The Solicitors' Accounts Rules 1991, reproduced in full as Appendix A, are intended to ensure the correct treatment of client's money, together with the implementation and maintenance of satisfactory accounting and recording systems. Detailed interpretation of the Rules can be found in *The Guide to the Professional Conduct of Solicitors 1996* and the *Solicitors' Accounts Manual* (6th edition). The aim of this guide is not to reproduce that interpretation but to consider what the Solicitors' Accounts Rules require in practice, and to provide guidance on the steps to be taken to ensure compliance. This, out of necessity, entails a concentration on client accounts, but certain areas have also been expanded to cover advice on possible ways of improving the general administration of the accounting function.

Chapter 1 sets the scene. It looks at what constitutes client's money, and deals with the establishment and operation of appropriate client accounts.

Chapter 2 identifies and explains each element of the books of account. It sets out, with the aid of some typical examples, the basic records that are required and are common to all systems.

The accounting systems and procedures that firms can utilise are detailed in **Chapter 3**. All aspects of receipts and payments are covered, as are billing arrangements, accounting for deposit interest, the treatment of commissions, and control processes such as reconciliations.

Once accounting systems and procedures have been established, there are still ongoing responsibilities for various members of the firm with regard to the continuing maintenance of the books of account and supervision of the accounting function. The final chapter, **Chapter 4**, deals with these areas and other related matters such as the appointment of book-keeping staff, training and security controls.

The book has been pitched at a level that assumes little prior knowledge (beyond the basics of double entry book-keeping and some understanding of the working of a solicitor's practice) and seeks to address even the simplest and most obvious of points. However, the intention throughout has been to promote high standards,

INTRODUCTION

sometimes with resultant resource implications but, hopefully, with consequential savings accruing from the avoidance of problems and costly remedial action. With this in mind, although firms must take the steps required to ensure compliance with the Rules, they may wish to concentrate on those additional aspects of the accounts that are most relevant and important to them.

Overall, while this is not an exhaustive examination of all of the systems and controls available, the principles involved are applicable to both manual and computer systems, and it is hoped that this guide will assist any firm in the development and improvement of its accounting operations.

CHAPTER 1
Setting Up and Using the Client Account

One of the basic principles behind the Solicitors' Accounts Rules is that client's money must be kept separate from office money. This necessitates the opening of a separate account or accounts to hold client's money.

1.1 WHAT IS 'CLIENT'S MONEY'?

The Solicitors' Accounts Rules 1991 define 'client's money' as 'money held or received by a solicitor on account of a person for whom he or she is acting in relation to the holding or receipt of such money either as a solicitor or, in connection with his or her practice as a solicitor, as agent, bailee, stakeholder or in any other capacity; provided that the expression "client's money" shall not include:

– money held or received on account of the trustees of a trust of which the solicitor is a controlled trustee; or

– money to which the only person entitled is the solicitor himself or herself or, in the case of a firm of solicitors, one or more of the partners in the firm.'

There are some common misconceptions about what is and what is not 'client's money'. It is important to remember that:

– Sums received by a solicitor on account of costs generally should be paid into a client account, and may not be transferred to office account until the provisions of Rule 7(a)(iv) have been complied with. This Rule requires that, before costs can be transferred from client account to office account, a bill of costs or other written intimation of the amount of costs incurred should be delivered to the client, and it should be made clear to the client in writing that the money held for him or her in the client account is to be applied towards or in satisfaction of such costs.

The money held in client account will, where appropriate, continue to earn interest for the client until it is transferred (see para. 3.5).

1

- In particular it should be noted that sums received by a solicitor in respect of stamp duty and Land Registry registration fees yet to be incurred are client's money, and must be paid into a client account.

- A solicitor cannot treat himself or herself as a client. Consequently, a principal may not conduct his or her personal or office transactions through a client account even if the firm is acting for the principal. However, if the firm is acting for a principal and some other person, for example a spouse (not being a principal), the firm is acting for both of them, and the matter must be conducted through a client account. Similarly, if the matter is a conveyancing transaction and the firm is also acting for a building society or other lender, that part of the transaction involving the lender's money should be dealt with through a client account.

   Where a firm conducts a conveyancing transaction on behalf of an assistant solicitor, the assistant solicitor should be treated as a client, and any monies should be kept in client account, even if it is the assistant solicitor who is handling the matter personally.

- The Solicitors' Accounts (Legal Aid Temporary Provision) Rule 1992 (reproduced as Appendix B) allows payments from the Legal Aid Board in respect of costs, all or part of which relate to unpaid fees of another lawyer, professional or other agent, or expert instructed by the solicitor, to be paid *en bloc* into office account, provided that any such fees that remain unpaid after 14 days are then transferred to client account.

   Subject to this provision, money received in respect of unpaid professional disbursements, being client's money, should be placed in client account.

- Interest earned on a general client account belongs to the solicitor, and should be paid directly into an office account by the bank. Note that bank charges levied by the bank in connection with the maintenance of the account should be paid from office account, and instructions must be given to the bank to this effect.

- A solicitor who receives client's money must pay it into a client account 'without delay'. In normal circumstances, this means on either the day of receipt or the next working day.

- Generally, commissions received in the course of a client retainer are client's money and therefore should be paid into client account. This is subject to some exceptions which are dealt with in para. 3.6.

SETTING UP AND USING THE CLIENT ACCOUNT

1.2 What is a 'Client Account'?

'Client account' is defined as 'a current or deposit account at a bank or deposit account with a building society in the name of the solicitor or his or her firm in the title of which the word "client" appears.'

Note that the definition does not include a building society share account. Therefore, if a building society account is to be opened to hold client's money, a deposit account should be opened. In addition, the Council of the Law Society regard it as essential that client's money is held in an instant access account so that it is immediately available, even though this may be at the sacrifice of interest.

All client accounts should be in the name of the firm or the solicitor in the case of a sole principal, and should have the word 'client' in the title. The word 'client' should appear in full and may not be abbreviated.

If, however, a client gives specific instructions that his or her money should not be placed in a client account, those instructions override the Solicitors' Accounts Rules and should be followed. Such instructions should be in writing or acknowledged by the solicitor to the client in writing.

Therefore, if a client gives instructions that his or her money is to be held in a building society share account, those instructions should be followed. In this case, the word 'client' should not be included in the title of the account as it cannot be a client account, even though it contains client's money. Nonetheless, the record-keeping requirements, etc., in respect of such accounts are the same as for other client's money. In particular, the funds contained in the accounts should be brought into the five-weekly reconciliation required by Rule 11(5).

The position is the same if a client gives instructions that his or her money is to be held in any other account that is not permitted to be used as a client account. So, for example, if a client gives instructions that his or her money is to be held in an account that is not instantly accessible, or in an offshore account, the instructions should be in writing or acknowledged by the solicitor to the client in writing, the word 'client' should not be included in the title of the account and the account must be brought into the reconciliation.

If a client gives instructions that funds held on his or her behalf be held in cash, again the instructions should be in writing or acknowledged in writing, and the funds must be brought into the reconciliation.

3

1.3 Signatories to the Client Account

Rule 11(6) defines the persons authorised by the Rules to sign client account cheques and other authorities for the withdrawal of funds from client accounts. The authorised persons are:

- a solicitor who holds a current practising certificate; or

- an employee of such a solicitor being either a solicitor or a Fellow of the Institute of Legal Executives who is confirmed by the Institute as being of good standing and who shall have been admitted a Fellow for not less than three years;

- a registered foreign lawyer who is a partner or director of the practice;

- in the case of an office dealing solely with conveyancing, an employee of such a solicitor being a licensed conveyancer.

It is permissible for unauthorised persons to appear on the mandate as long as any cheques or other withdrawal authorities signed by them are countersigned by an authorised person.

1.4 Paid Cheques

Rule 11(9)(b)(i) provides that a solicitor should retain all paid cheques for a period of at least two years, unless he or she has arranged with the relevant bank or building society *in writing* that the bank or building society will retain the paid cheques for the requisite period. If the latter course of action is taken, it should be ensured that the necessary confirmation is obtained and kept.

1.5 Separate Designated Accounts

Rather than hold the monies of a particular client in the general client account, a separate designated account may be opened into which is paid only money held on behalf of the particular client. Again, note that the definition of a 'separate designated account' does not include a building society share account.

All the Rules applicable to general client accounts are also applicable to separate designated accounts. In particular, all separate designated accounts should be reconciled at least once every five weeks in accordance with Rule 11(5), and the title of each such account should contain the word 'client'. In addition, each account should be designated by reference to the identity of the client or matter concerned. It is recommended that the client's name is used to designate the account, as this provides for ready identification.

1.6 Checking Statements

It is recommended that bank and building society statements are checked against the entries made in the books of account as soon as possible after the statements have been received. The more frequently this is done, the easier it will be to trace any errors that may have occurred.

The statements should be checked to ensure that interest on the general client account has not been credited to that account, and that bank charges have not been withdrawn from client account in error. It should also be verified that accounts have been designated correctly.

When conducting the reconciliation in respect of separate designated accounts, it is sufficient to use the last statement received only if there has been no movement on the account since it was received. If there has been any movement, whether in respect of interest credited or of any other movement, an up-to-date statement should be obtained and compared. General client account statements should be received at least monthly. It may be appropriate for them to be received more often depending on the volume of transactions through the account.

1.7 Controlled Trust Accounts

Part II of the Solicitors' Accounts Rules deals with controlled trusts. A 'controlled trust' in relation to a solicitor shall mean a trust of which he or she is a controlled trustee.

A 'controlled trustee' is defined as a solicitor who is a sole trustee or co-trustee only with one or more of his or her partners or employees. The expression 'trustee' includes a personal representative. If any one of the firm's solicitors is the only trustee, this will be a controlled trust. However, if a non-solicitor employee is the only trustee, this will not be a controlled trust. In the case of a trust with more than one trustee, if all of the trustees are employees, whether solicitors or not, this will not be a controlled trust.

If a former partner who remains with the firm as a retired, non-practising consultant is the sole trustee, acting in the capacity of a professional trustee and charging as such, this will be a controlled trust. In this case the consultant should have a practising certificate, and indemnity cover should be in place unless Rule

29 of the Solicitors' Indemnity Rules 1995 applies. The consultant will be required to deliver an Accountant's Report because he or she is holding controlled trust money although a dispensation from this requirement may be granted in limited circumstances. To avoid these requirements the consultant should cease to act or charge as a professional trustee.

If a former partner who remains with the firm as a retired, non-practising consultant is a trustee with one of the partners, this will be a controlled trust because the partner is a controlled trustee. If that consultant is a trustee with one of the firm's employees, whether a solicitor or not, this will not be a controlled trust.

Where a controlled trustee holds or receives trust money subject to a trust of which he or she is a controlled trustee, that money shall be paid into a controlled trust account, unless it is paid into a client account.

A 'controlled trust account' is defined as 'a current or deposit account kept at a bank or deposit account kept with a building society in the title of which the word "trustee" or "executor" appears, or which is otherwise clearly designated as a controlled trust account, and kept solely for money subject to a particular trust of which the solicitor is a controlled trustee'. This definition excludes the use of building society share accounts. However, note that the Rules cannot fetter a trustee's discretion at law to place money in, for example, a building society share account.

Rule 19 details the record-keeping obligations in relation to controlled trust accounts (see para. 2.9).

1.8 INTEREST

If funds are held on behalf of a client in a separate designated account, the interest to be paid to the client is the interest received on that account. In respect of funds held in general client account, it is important to be vigilant in identifying matters where the deposit interest provisions apply, and in paying the required amount of interest over to the client.

This is particularly so where funds are held for a client both in a general client account and in a separate designated account. If the funds held in the general client account are or have been such that the deposit interest provisions apply, then that interest should be paid over as well as the interest earned on the separate designated account.

Any agreement with a client that the solicitor is to keep all or part of the interest due to the client under the deposit interest provisions should be in writing.

Note that the deposit interest provisions do not apply to monies that are the subject of a controlled trust. In the case of a controlled trust, all interest earned must be accounted for in accordance with the principle of general law that precludes a solicitor who is a trustee from obtaining any benefit from the trust.

The deposit interest provisions are dealt with in greater detail in para. 3.5.

1.9 Funds Held Jointly with Third Parties

Money held in an account operated jointly with another firm of solicitors or a third party is not client's money, as it is not in the sole control of the firm. The word 'client' should not therefore appear in the title of any such account, and the funds should not be brought into the reconciliation, although as a matter of good practice separate records in memorandum form should be kept.

1.10 Enduring Powers of Attorney and Court of Protection

Where a solicitor as donee of a power of attorney opens an account in his or her name to hold the donor's money, then the account is a client account and is subject to the Solicitors' Accounts Rules. Therefore the account should conform to the requirements of a client account; it should be designated correctly, and full client account records should be maintained. Where a solicitor under a power of attorney merely operates an existing account in the client's name, it is not a client account and is not covered by the Solicitors' Accounts Rules, although as a matter of good practice it is recommended that the solicitor maintains separate records of such accounts in memorandum form. If a power of attorney is registered at a bank or building society, and the account at that point is redesignated into the solicitor's name, it will then become subject to the Solicitors' Accounts Rules.

If a solicitor is operating an existing account in the client's name under an enduring power of attorney, and the client subsequently becomes mentally incapable and the power is registered at the Court of Protection, no record-keeping obligations arise provided that the account remains in the client's name. If the account is redesignated into the solicitor's name, it becomes subject to the Solicitors' Accounts Rules.

Where a solicitor is appointed as receiver on behalf of a client by the Court of Protection and opens an account in his or her name to deal with the patient's monies, this constitutes a court appointment covered by a separate regulatory regime, and is not subject to the Solicitors' Accounts Rules.

CHAPTER 2
The Books of Account

The Solicitors' Accounts Rules have various specific requirements regarding the 'books of account', how they should be kept and what records should be retained. While these requirements remain the same, the manner in which they are achieved naturally varies to some extent, depending on the type of system used.

2.1 WHAT ARE THE BASIC REQUIREMENTS?

The starting point for any consideration of the books of account has to be 'double entry'. This means that for all bank and building society accounts, both office and client, there should be records in both a cash book and a ledger. These records need to be kept up to date at all times. This means writing up at least weekly in even the smallest practice and, in larger practices, daily. All client account ledgers should show a current balance, and it is preferable for a running balance to be maintained. It is also recommended that office account ledgers are kept to the same standard.

2.2 CASH BOOKS

The cash book is a chronological record of every financial transaction involving client's money. Alternative names that are commonly used are 'audit trail', 'transaction list', 'day book' and, confusingly, 'the client ledger'. Even where a number of client accounts are maintained, one cash book is sufficient, but in some circumstances separate cash books may be preferable, e.g. offices using different banks. The narrative used to describe transactions in the cash book should be sufficient to identify the source or destination of the money and the nature of the transaction. The narrative for mortgage advances should identify the lender concerned, and should state that the money is a mortgage advance. Also, money held by the solicitor as stakeholder needs to be identified as such in the narrative. It is also sensible to include the reference number of cheques or credit slips, and to maintain a record of the balance to assist in reconciliation.

2.3 Ledgers

A ledger is a chronological record of every financial transaction in connection with an individual client or a matter for an individual client. The entries are duplicates of those entries in the cash book that relate to that specific client or matter, and the same requirements for frequency and detail of posting apply. This is particularly the case where a mortgage advance is received, as Rule 11(3) requires the funds of both borrower and institutional lender to be clearly identifiable if a single client ledger is to be used. This effectively requires the narrative to refer to a mortgage advance and to identify the lender. Where money is held by the solicitor as stakeholder, this also should be made clear in the narrative.

2.4 Basic Systems

In their most basic form, the cash book and ledger will be written up separately. Typical examples of this are shown in Tables 2.4A and 2.4B.

2.5 Carbon Systems

To avoid the need to write up every transaction twice, a number of systems are available that use carbon paper to write up the cash book, on a large sheet, at the same time as the individual ledger is written up. These systems all work on a similar principle. The cash book is a large sheet mounted on a board. Each transaction is written on the relevant client ledger, which is positioned over the next line in the cash book, with the carbon paper producing the cash book entry.

2.6 Computer Systems

There are also a large number of computer systems of varying degrees of complexity, which will post entries to both the cash book and the ledgers automatically when the relevant information is input. Some systems restrict the amount of narrative that can be included and, with such systems, greater care is needed to ensure that a satisfactory narrative is recorded.

2.7 Deposit Accounts

Some ledgers have a facility to record money held on separate deposit. If the ledgers that are used do not have this facility, then a separate ledger will be needed for this money. These ledger entries will, of course, require their matching double entry. This is normally automatic on computer systems, but otherwise this

THE BOOKS OF ACCOUNT

TABLE 2.4A CLIENTS' CASH BOOK

Date	Cheque/ C-Foil number	Client name	Narrative	Debit (Receipt) £	Credit (Payment) £	Balance £
			Balance b/fwd			13,000.00
5/8/94	537	Campbell Decd	Halifax B. Soc closure of A/C	10,000.00		23,000.00
8/8/94	114	Anderson	Stamp duty – Inland Revenue		1,200.00	21,800.00
10/8/94	115	Anderson	Estate agent's fees – Bloggs & Co		750.00	21,050.00
14/8/94	538	Baker	Payment on A/C of costs – of you	500.00		21,550.00
14/8/94	539	Martin	Receipt of damages – Municipal Mutual	3,000.00		24,550.00
17/8/94	116	Jenkins	Local search – Hundred Acre Wood D.C.		700.00	24,480.00
19/8/94	117	Reed	Medical report fee – Dr Brown		150.00	24,330.00
22/8/94	540	Yorick Decd	Close A/C – Stratford Savings Bank	6,807.23		31,137.23
22/8/94	118	Yorick Decd	Pay funeral A/C – Cassius & Son		1,145.62	29,991.61
22/8/94	119	Yorick Decd	Pay council tax – Stratford D.C.		4.76	29,986.85
22/8/94	120	Yorick Decd	Valuation fee – Shylock & Co		47.00	29,939.85
22/8/94	–	Yorick Decd	Client office tfr – Disbs		210.85	29,729.00
22/8/94	–	Yorick Decd	Trf to deposit – Stratford Savings Bank		5,399.00	24,330.00
24/8/94	541	Jones	On A/C of disbs	100.00		24,430.00
25/8/94	–	Roberts	Client office tfr – Costs		1,175.00	23,255.00
27/8/94	121	Jones	Local search – Stratford D.C.		70.00	23,185.00
28/8/94	122	Evans	Stamp duty – Inland Revenue		800.00	22,385.00
31/8/94	542	Smith	Deposit – of you	2,000.00		24,385.00

11

COMPLYING WITH THE SOLICITORS' ACCOUNTS RULES: A PRACTICAL GUIDE

TABLE 2.4B CLIENT'S LEDGER

Client: Christopher Yorick Deceased

Date	Details	Office Debit £	Office Credit £	Office Balance £	Client Debit £	Client Credit £	Client Balance £
1/7/94	Cash found at house					38.40	38.40
3/7/94	Stat notice fee – London Gazette	35.25		35.25			
3/7/94	Stat notice fee – Dunsinane Echo	58.75		94.00			
5/7/94	Client office tfr – Disbs		38.40	55.60	38.40		Nil
22/7/94	Petty cash – Swearing fee	4.50		60.10			
24/7/94	HMPG probate fee	150.75		210.85			
22/8/94	Stratford Savings Bank – Close A/C					6,807.23	6,807.23
22/8/94	Cassius & Son funeral A/C				1,145.62		5,661.61
22/8/94	Stratford D.C. – Council Tax				4.76		5,656.85
22/8/94	Shylock & Co valuation fee				47.00		5,609.85
22/8/94	Client – Office trf – Disb		210.85	Nil	210.85		5,399.00
22/8/94	Trf to Stratford Savings Bank – Deposit				5,399.00		Nil
14/10/94	Portia & Co – Deposit on Glamis Court Stakeholder					6,800.00	6,800.00
14/10/94	Stratford Savings Bank trf to Deposit				6,800.00		Nil
28/10/94	Portia & Co – Balance on Glamis Court					61,200.00	61,200.00
28/10/94	Bill 426	850.00		850.00			
28/10/94	VAT	148.75		998.75			
28/10/94	Stratford Savings Bank from Deposit					12,252.99	73,452.99
28/10/94	Augustus – Legacy				2,000.00		71,452.99
28/10/94	Anthony – Legacy				2,000.00		69,452.99
28/10/94	Falstaff – Legacy				68,454.24		998.75
28/10/94	Client – Office tfr – Costs		998.75	Nil	998.75		Nil

12

should be made in a separate combined cash book for such accounts. With many of the carbon systems, this will merely need a different sheet to be placed under the ledger. The procedures used are therefore the same as those used for the general client account, with every transaction, such as the addition of interest, appearing both in the cash book and on the specific ledger. Where money is transferred between general client account and separate designated accounts, entries will need to be made in both cash books [Rules 11(1) and 11(2)].

Table 2.7A shows transactions that commonly arise with such accounts, i.e. a transfer from general client account followed by the accrual of interest and finally a transfer back to general client account prior to payment to the client.

2.8 Inter-Client Transfers

As client-to-client transfers do not involve a movement of funds at the bank, there will be no corresponding entry in the cash book. It is therefore necessary to maintain an independent record in the form of a transfer journal. A typical transfer journal would appear as follows:

TRANSFER JOURNAL

Date	Narrative	Debit (Receipt) £	Credit (Payment) £
1/2/95	Debit Client Smith A.	100	
1/2/95	Credit Client Smith B.		100

Memo: Being correction of posting error on 31/1/95 where receipt of funds in respect of A. Smith was incorrectly allocated to B. Smith.

Firms may wish to make contra entries in the cash book as an alternative to maintaining a transfer journal.

2.9 Controlled Trusts

Money held or received in connection with a controlled trust is now dealt with by the Solicitors' Accounts Rules, rather than separately under the Solicitors' Trust Accounts Rules as before (see para. 1.7). Such money should be paid into a controlled trust account unless it is paid into client account. If it is paid into client account, the normal book-keeping requirements for client's money apply. If the money is paid into a controlled trust account, the bank statement or passbook will

TABLE 2.7A

Client: Christopher Yorick Deceased separate designated account

Date	Details	Office Debit £	Office Credit £	Office Balance £	Client Debit £	Client Credit £	Client Balance £
22/8/94	Tfr from Client A/C					5,399.00	5,399.00
14/10/94	Tfr from Client A/C Stakeholder					6,800.00	12,199.00
28/10/94	Interest to close					53.99	12,252.99
28/10/94	Tfr to Client A/C				12,252.99		Nil

often be a sufficient accounting record. However, if the matter is more complex, a formal ledger should be maintained. Where controlled trust accounts are used, either these should be kept together centrally, e.g. by retaining all statements and/or passbooks in the Accounts Department, or a central register of them should be maintained [Rule 19].

2.10 Reconciliation

If all entries are made promptly and accurately, then the books of account should balance. The Solicitors' Accounts Rules require a check of this, effectively once a month, called the reconciliation. Not only does this require a comparison of the total of all client ledger balances (including separate deposit accounts) with the cash book balances, bank statements and building society passbooks, but also the preparation and retention of a written statement showing these comparisons, including the reasons for any differences [Rule 11(5)]. Reconciliations are considered in more detail in para. 3.4.

2.11 What Other Records are Required?

The Solicitors' Accounts Rules require various other items to be retained or other records to be made. Items normally have to be retained for six years, except authorities to withdraw money from client account. The first of these requirements is that all bills and written intimations of costs need to be recorded in a bills delivered book or that a file of copy bills and written intimations should be retained.

It is also necessary to retain either the original or copies of all the signed authorities for withdrawing money from client account. The retention period for these is two years. Cheques and telegraphic transfer requests are the most obvious forms of these, but others include requests to close accounts or to transfer money between accounts. Many firms rely on their banks to retain paid cheques. While this is perfectly acceptable, the arrangement should be confirmed in writing, with the confirmation being retained by the firm. For all other withdrawals from client account, the responsibility for retention rests with the firm, and copies of all signed authorities should be retained, ideally in the Accounts Department.

Bank statements are relatively obvious items to retain, but other items that should also be retained include cheque stubs (including cancelled/spoiled cheques), paying-in counterfoils, transfer request counterfoils, and debit/credit slips if used. As the entries in the books of account are made from these items, in order to maintain full, detailed records of all payments and receipts, it is essential that such items, e.g. cheque book stubs, should be fully completed with all details when written out. The necessary details are the date, the account, the payer or payee and what the payment represents. Likewise, if a 'slip' or 'chit' system is used, similar details should be recorded on these [Rules 11(4), 11(6) and 11(7)].

2.12 Solicitors' Investment Business Rules

Additional record-keeping requirements relating to accounts apply to firms which hold investment business certificates. The Solicitors' Investment Business Rules 1990 have been replaced by the Solicitors' Investment Business Rules 1995 which came into force on 1 June 1996. Under Rule 13 of the 1990 Rules, bills for discrete investment business should be separate from bills relating to other work, or should show the discrete investment business element separately. Such bills are also required to be retained in a separate bills delivered book or file of copy bills, or in a separate part of the main one. Rule 26 is the equivalent Rule in the Solicitors' Investment Business Rules 1995. This Rule is, in substance, the same as the 1990 Rule save that it no longer refers to a separate bills delivered book but merely requires such bills to be identified or recorded separately from other bills.

The Solicitors' Investment Business Rules 1995 have introduced an additional record-keeping requirement in relation to the receipt of commissions. With effect from 1 June 1996, firms are required to keep a record of the total amount of commissions received which are attributable to investment business and the total amount of such commissions which are not paid or credited to clients [Rule 14, Solicitors' Investment Business Rules 1995].

2.13 Any Other Points to Note?

The Solicitors' Accounts Rules require some arrangements or instructions to be in writing or to be confirmed in writing. It is therefore advisable to have the confirmation of such arrangements or instructions retained centrally. Examples of these are:

- instructions to withhold money from client account [Rule 9(2)];
- private loan agreements between clients [Rule 10(2)];
- arrangements for the bank to retain paid client account cheques [Rule 11(9)];
- the client's agreement to the retention of commission in excess of £20, together with a copy of the corresponding commission disclosure document [Solicitors' Practice Rule 10].

CHAPTER 3
General Accounting Systems

This chapter considers the systems that firms of solicitors can operate in order to improve compliance with the Solicitors' Accounts Rules, and which will enable the financial aspects of a practice to be administered effectively.

3.1 MONEY RECEIVED

It is important to ensure that all client's money is paid promptly into a client account. However, note that where a solicitor receives a cheque or draft to be held to the sender's order, it must not be presented for payment without the sender's consent. By contrast, money sent by telegraphic transfer to be held to the sender's order must be held in client account. Where a solicitor receives a cheque payable to a third party that he or she then forwards on, this does not constitute client's money and is therefore not subject to the Accounts Rules.

3.1.1 Post received

It is regarded as good practice for more than one responsible member of staff to open incoming mail at a central collection point, with the post then being reviewed by a principal prior to its distribution to the appropriate fee earners. As well as enabling principals to monitor incoming post, this procedure can also assist in the indirect supervision of fee earners.

3.1.2 Receipt of client account cheques

Where practices have more than one fee earner, it is recommended that a day book is used to record the receipt of incoming cheques, prior to their distribution to the fee earners.

The Accounts Department will need to compare cheques returned to them by the fee earners for banking, with the day book entries. This will help to ensure that cheques received by the practice during the course of the day are recorded correctly, and that the cheques passed to fee earners are returned to the Accounts Department promptly.

In situations where cheques received are passed directly to the Accounts Department, it should not be necessary to maintain a day book. A note of the receipt of cheques should, however, be made on the relevant correspondence in order to inform fee earners.

Where cheques are passed to the relevant fee earners, it is important to ensure that when these are sent to the Accounts Department for banking they are accompanied by the appropriate posting information. This may be achieved by the use of a posting slip, which should be completed in duplicate, with the original and cheque being passed promptly to a central collection point in the Accounts Department and a copy being retained on the appropriate client's file for reference.

A suggested format for a posting slip is illustrated below:

CLIENT/OFFICE RECEIPT

[DELETE AS APPROPRIATE]

DATE:
CLIENT'S NAME:
MATTER NUMBER:
DETAIL:

AMOUNT: £　　　　　　　　FEE EARNER:　　　　　　[INITIAL]

It is advisable for the relevant fee earner to complete the posting slip because of the difficulties that can arise when distinguishing between client's and office money. Particular effort should be made to ensure that these slips are completed as accurately and clearly as possible, and attention should be paid to the requirements of Rule 11(3) regarding mortgage advances, and also the need to identify stakeholder deposits.

The following paragraphs will assume the use of the posting slip where appropriate.

3.1.3 Receipt of cash

When cash is received from a client, particularly a large amount, consideration should always be given to the Money Laundering Regulations (see para. 4.6.6).

Any cash receipts should be counted in the presence of the client by the relevant fee earner and another member of staff. Care should be taken to check for any forged bank notes.

A receipt should be issued to the client, and the client's signature should be obtained. A copy of the receipt should be retained on a central file. A posting slip should then be completed in the same manner as for cheques, but should specify that the sum was received in cash. The cash, together with the posting slip, should immediately be passed to the Accounts Department for banking that day.

3.1.4 Client account banking

Rule 3 of the Solicitors' Accounts Rules requires client's money to be paid into a client account without delay. This means on either the day of receipt or at least the next working day.

Any cash received should be banked immediately. If it is received outside normal working hours, it needs to be stored securely, or special arrangements should be made with the bank.

The banking slips/paying-in book should be prepared by a responsible member of staff, and, where practicable, verified by another employee before delivery to the bank. If the banking includes a significant amount of cash, consideration should be given to security: for example, delivery by more than one member of staff, varying the time when bankings are made, and appropriate insurance cover.

3.2 Money Paid Out

Before a payment is made on behalf of a client, a check should be made to ensure that sufficient funds are held in client account on behalf of that client.

3.2.1 Cleared funds

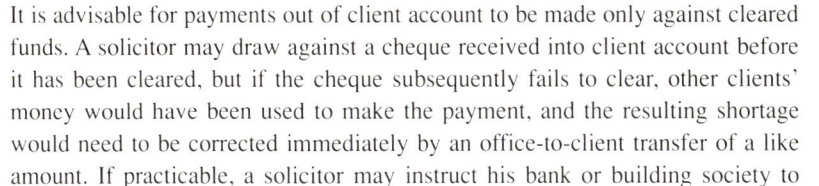

It is advisable for payments out of client account to be made only against cleared funds. A solicitor may draw against a cheque received into client account before it has been cleared, but if the cheque subsequently fails to clear, other clients' money would have been used to make the payment, and the resulting shortage would need to be corrected immediately by an office-to-client transfer of a like amount. If practicable, a solicitor may instruct his bank or building society to charge all unpaid client account credits to his office account.

3.2.2 Client account cheques

Where a client account cheque is required, the principal or fee earner should complete a cheque requisition slip in duplicate; the original should be passed to the Accounts Department together with the corresponding letter, and the copy should be retained on the client's file.

A suggested format for a cheque requisition posting slip is illustrated below:

CLIENT/OFFICE CHEQUE REQUISITION

[DELETE AS APPROPRIATE]

DATE:
CLIENT'S NAME:
MATTER NUMBER:
PAYEE:
DETAIL:

AMOUNT: £   FEE EARNER: [INITIAL]

It is advisable for only a limited number of staff, who would generally be members of the Accounts Department, to prepare cheques.

Prior to a cheque being raised, either the fee earner or the person responsible for writing the cheque should ensure that there are sufficient funds held on behalf of that client, by reference to the client's ledger account. The use of a running balance on each client's ledger will assist in this respect. When completed, cheques should be passed to authorised signatories [see Rule 11(6)] together with any accompanying correspondence. The cheques should then be passed to the relevant fee earners (who can check the details) immediately prior to dispatch of the post, ensuring that signed client account cheques are not held insecurely for any longer than necessary. Firms may also wish to consider using two signatories for large client account cheques.

The following additional points should also be considered:

– All cheque books should be kept securely, and should be marked clearly as either office or client account on the front cover.

- If practicable, only one cheque book should be used at any one time, and cheques should be completed in sequential order. This is particularly important when coming to the end of a cheque book and starting a new one.

- All client account cheques should be crossed 'account payee'.

- To protect client account cheques made payable to banks or building societies against cheque fraud, the client's name or account number with that bank or building society should be included in the cheque.

- It is generally inadvisable to issue client account 'cash' or 'bearer' cheques without taking appropriate precautions. These could include obtaining a signed receipt from the client, or accompanying the client to the bank to cash the cheque.

- Any spoilt cheques should be retained by the firm. They should be clearly marked as cancelled, and the signature should be obliterated.

- Where instructions are given to a bank or building society to cancel a client account cheque, a copy of those instructions together with the bank or building society's confirmation that this has been done should be retained.

3.2.3 Withdrawal of cash

The following points should be considered when withdrawing client's money in cash:

- A posting slip should be completed in duplicate by the fee earner. The original should be passed to the Accounts Department and the copy retained on the client's file. The posting slip should indicate why cash is required.

- The fee earner should seek the client's written authority to make a withdrawal by cash, and a copy of that authority should be passed to the Accounts Department and retained on a central file.

- The cash should be counted by the fee earner in the presence of the client/recipient and another member of the firm.

- A signed receipt should be obtained and a copy passed to the Accounts Department for retention on a central file.

- Particular attention should be paid to security when withdrawing cash from the bank.

– It is a breach of the Accounts Rules to have client petty cash, as all client's money should be held in a client account at a bank or building society. Petty cash will usually be required only in respect of office expenditure, though it may be used to pay disbursements on behalf of a client, e.g. oath fees.

3.2.4 Telegraphic transfers

Prior to requesting a telegraphic transfer withdrawal from a client account, the fee earner should check with the Accounts Department that any necessary incoming funds have been confirmed by the bank as having been received. It is not sufficient to rely upon an assurance from the paying solicitor that the transfer of funds has been authorised, because if the payment is not subsequently received, other clients' money will have been used in breach of the Rules.

Telegraphic transfer requisition posting slips should be completed in duplicate by the fee earner and should include the bank details of the receiving party.

If the telegraphic transfer instructions to the bank are given by way of letter, this should be prepared by the relevant fee earner and passed to the book-keeper with the corresponding posting slip. Where a standard bank form is used, this should be completed by the Accounts Department on receipt of the posting slip.

The letter of instruction or standard bank form should then be passed to an authorised signatory [see Rule 11(6)] for signature. The signed authority should then be copied and a copy retained by the firm for at least two years in accordance with the requirements of Rule 11(9)(b)(ii). It is advisable to retain a copy both on the client's file and on a central file in the Accounts Department. The letter or standard bank form authorising the transfer should then be delivered to the bank either by hand or by facsimile transmission.

Where instructions to effect telegraphic transfers are given by telephone, it is necessary to ensure that a letter of instruction or standard bank form has been completed and signed before the instructions are given. A copy of the signed authority should be retained by the firm and the original forwarded to the bank by way of confirmation.

Uncompleted telegraphic transfer forms should be retained in a secure place, and should never be signed blank.

Where instructions are given by telephone, consideration should be given to security issues, such as the use of regularly changed codes and the implementation of call-back systems (see para. 4.6.3). The bank or building society may also be consulted regarding other security procedures that could be adopted.

3.2.5 Client-to-office transfers

Fee earners should prepare a transfer instruction posting slip in duplicate, with the original being passed to the Accounts Department and the copy retained on the client's file. This slip should refer to bill numbers, and should provide complete details of any disbursements to which the transfer relates. A full breakdown of disbursements on the posting slip will aid the Accounts Department in identifying transfers in respect of unpaid disbursements in breach of the Solicitors' Accounts Rules.

A suggested format for a transfer instruction posting slip is illustrated below:

```
CLIENT-TO-OFFICE TRANSFER INSTRUCTION

DATE:
CLIENT'S NAME:
MATTER NUMBER:
DETAIL:                        £
        BILL OF COSTS:
        DISB. PAID
        DISB. UNPAID
                              _____
TOTAL TRANSFER
                              _____
BILL REF:              FEE EARNER:            [INITIAL]
```

Before transferring any money from client account in respect of costs, the Accounts Department should verify with the relevant fee earner that a corresponding bill or other written intimation of costs has been delivered to the client in accordance with Rule 7(a)(iv).

Instructions to the bank or building society to authorise a transfer from client to office account should be passed by the Accounts Department to an authorised signatory for signing, and a copy of the signed authority should be retained for at least two years in accordance with Rule 11(9)(b)(ii).

It is usually the case that client-to-office transfers relate to a number of clients. It is therefore important that appropriate records are maintained to enable individual client-to-office transfers to be identified.

Where a firm can effect transfers from client account using a terminal provided by the bankers, care should be taken to ensure that an authority signed by an authorised signatory is in place before a transfer is made, notwithstanding that the bank may not require a written authority for their purposes. Depending on the requirements of the bank, either the signed authority or a copy of it should be retained for at least two years.

3.2.6 Client-to-client transfers

The transfer of funds from the ledger account of one client to the ledger account of another client should normally only be necessary in respect of related matters or transactions.

Where a client-to-client transfer is required, the fee earner should complete a transfer authority posting slip in duplicate. The original should be passed to the Accounts Department and copies retained on the appropriate clients' files. Full details of the reason for the transfer should be included on the posting slip, and details of the transfer should be entered in the transfer journal (see para. 2.8).

A suggested format for a transfer instruction posting slip is illustrated below:

CLIENT-TO-CLIENT TRANSFER INSTRUCTION

DATE:
TRANSFEROR: CLIENT'S NAME:
              MATTER NUMBER:
TRANSFEREE: CLIENT'S NAME:
              MATTER NUMBER:
DETAILS:

AMOUNT: £   FEE EARNER: [INITIAL]

As a withdrawal of money is not being made from a client account, such transfers do not need to be authorised in accordance with Rule 11(6). However, endorsement by an authorised signatory is recommended. Client-to-client transfers should be kept under review, and any transfers between unrelated matters investigated.

Where a transfer is made in respect of a private loan from one client to another, the written authority of the lender should be obtained prior to the transfer taking place [see Rule 10(2)], and it is advisable to retain such authorities on a central file.

3.3 Treatment of Costs

3.3.1 Raising and delivering bills

When drafting a bill of costs, fee earners should ensure that the narrative on that bill is as detailed as possible. In accordance with the requirements of section 67 of the Solicitors Act 1974, the bill should identify as unpaid any disbursements that have not been paid before delivery of the bill. Note that an application to the Legal Aid Board for a payment on account of costs is regarded as an interim bill or written intimation of costs, and needs to be dealt with accordingly.

A bill or other written intimation of costs should be delivered to the client before, or at least at the same time as, a transfer takes place, in accordance with Rule 7(a)(iv). Procedures should be adopted to verify that bills have been delivered to clients before transfers take place; if the Accounts Department have not already been advised that a bill has been delivered, they should seek confirmation that this has been done before transferring the costs. Note that an action may not be brought to recover any costs due to a solicitor unless, inter alia, a bill signed by the sole practitioner or a partner in the firm has been delivered to the client (see section 69 of the Solicitors Act 1974).

A periodic review of the bills delivered book or copy bills file should be made to identify credit notes that reverse bills of costs. These should be rare and, where they arise, should be investigated. Where a credit note is properly raised, a solicitor should also deliver this to his or her client.

3.3.2 Recording and posting of bills delivered

In accordance with the requirements of Rule 11(4), a solicitor should maintain either a bills delivered book or a file of copy bills delivered. In both instances these will need to include any other written intimations of costs that have been sent to clients.

It is also recommended that a copy of the bill or other written intimation is kept on the client's file, particularly where a bills delivered book is maintained. In addition, consideration should be given to retaining copy completion statements with corresponding copy bills, and it is prudent for Accounts Department staff to verify completion statements prior to their issue.

From a record-keeping point of view, bills of costs should be posted to clients' ledgers when rendered. Where firms account for VAT on a 'cash accounting basis' (i.e. output VAT is determined by reference to the date of receipt of payment rather than the date of the bill of costs), bills of costs should still be posted to the ledgers when rendered. Here, however, separate records will need to be maintained for VAT purposes, as the bills posted to the ledgers in a particular period will not accord with the bills that are relevant in determining the VAT liability for that period (i.e. those that have been paid). The amount posted will only reflect the profit costs and VAT elements of the bill, as disbursements should be posted to clients' ledgers when paid. Any VAT implications that may arise with regard to the rendering and posting of bills should be discussed with the firm's accountant.

3.3.3 Receipt of costs

Where money is received in respect of a bill of costs and/or disbursements paid on behalf of a client, the receipt should be paid directly into the office account unless paid into a client account under Rule 5A. If costs are paid into client account they should be transferred to office account within seven days of receipt.

Where a cheque is received from a client, part of which relates to money due to the firm and part of which constitutes client's money, either the cheque should be split, by arrangement with the bank, or the whole amount should be paid into the client account. The part that relates to office money should then be transferred to the office account as soon as possible.

Money may only be transferred or paid into office account in respect of disbursements, e.g. professional disbursements, Land Registry fees and stamp duty, where these have actually been paid out of office account. In the case of disbursements paid by means of a credit account, these may be withdrawn as soon as the liability has been incurred.

Money received on account of costs should be paid into client account, except in the case of agreed fees, where it should be paid into the office account. Note that sums held in client account in respect of untransferred costs and payments on account of costs constitute client's money, and will continue to earn interest, where appropriate, for the client until transferred.

Where a cheque is received in respect of a bill of costs, this should be passed to the fee earner, who should advise the Accounts Department if any element of the receipt relates to unpaid disbursements. If in doubt, the whole payment should be made to the client account, and any sums due to the office account should be transferred in accordance with the above provisions.

Unpaid bills should be reviewed regularly and followed up by the fee earners. The separate filing of paid and unpaid bills can aid in this process. A review of the monthly clients' matter listing can also be effective in identifying money that is held in client account which can properly be transferred to the office account in respect of costs and paid disbursements.

3.3.4 Costs received from the Legal Aid Board

The Solicitors' Accounts (Legal Aid Temporary Provision) Rule 1992 (see Appendix B) provides that costs received from the Legal Aid Board containing money on account of unpaid disbursements may be paid into office account, provided those disbursements are paid within 14 days of receipt. Any disbursements that are not so paid should be transferred to the client account within 14 days of receipt. It is therefore imperative that any unpaid disbursements are identified on receipt, and that fee earners are notified accordingly. If fee earners do not issue instructions that disbursements are to be paid immediately, the Accounts Department will need to monitor the situation, and if instructions are not received within the 14 day period, a transfer will need to be made to the client account. Firms may consider the immediate transfer of all sums received from the Legal Aid Board in respect of unpaid disbursements to client account in order to avoid a breach of this Rule.

The above Rule applies to payments made by the Legal Aid Board in respect of civil litigation matters and where a client is legally aided in a magistrates' court case and the firm applies to the Board for payment. This Rule does not, however, apply to payments of costs made by the Crown Court, which are paid out of central funds.

Difficulties may arise where money is due back to the Legal Aid Board in respect of a legally aided matter, e.g. where the firm's costs are settled in full by a third party and the firm has already received a payment on account of costs from the Legal Aid Board. In these circumstances, the payment from the third party is a mixed payment. If the cheque is not split it should be paid into client account and only the balance transferred to office account after deducting the amount already paid by the Legal Aid Board including any green form payment. The money due back to the Board should be transferred to a Legal Aid Board suspense ledger and retained on client account pending recoupment by the Board from the next payment due to the firm from the Board. One advantage of maintaining a Legal Aid Board suspense ledger is that the solicitor can see at a glance the total amount of money due to the Board. Note that deposit interest will not be payable in respect of this money. Although money held by a solicitor on behalf of the Legal Aid Board falls within the definition of client's money, the Legal Aid Board is not a client for the purposes of the deposit interest provisions. Therefore money held on its behalf will not be subject to these provisions (see para. 3.5).

3.4 Client Account Reconciliations

3.4.1 Requirements under Rule 11(5)

The above Rule requires:

– a comparison to be made of the clients' cash book balance with the corresponding clients' bank balance after allowing for unpresented items;

– a comparison of the clients' cash book balance with the total of the clients' matter balances.

The above comparisons need to be undertaken at least once every five weeks, in effect monthly, and a reconciliation statement showing the cause of any differences must be produced and retained for at least six years. It is vital to ensure that each of the figures required for the above comparisons relates to the same date.

The purpose of the above Rule is to verify that sufficient funds are held in client account to meet the firm's liabilities to clients, and to identify any posting or bank errors.

3.4.2 Clients' bank reconciliation statement

The final balance on a bank statement is unlikely to be the same as that shown in the accounting records. Any discrepancy may be attributable to receipts, cheques paid or transfers included in the firm's records but which have not yet cleared through the bank account at the reconciliation date. In order to agree the bank balance to the accounting records, it is therefore necessary to ascertain those receipts and payments included in the books of account but not yet transacted at the bank.

To identify any unpresented or outstanding items, cash book postings should be ticked off to the corresponding bank statement entries in the period to be reconciled, and both cash book and bank statements should be marked accordingly.

It is then necessary to refer back to the previous period's bank reconciliation statement to identify those items that were unpresented or outstanding at that time and which remain uncleared at the bank at the date of the current reconciliation. Again, it is necessary to tick off the previous period's uncleared items to this period's bank statement entries in order to identify those outstanding or unpresented items that need to be included in this period's reconciliation statement.

Any items included on the bank statement but not in the cash book should be noted, as the cash book balance may need to be adjusted accordingly. Bank errors should, however, be adjusted on the bank reconciliation statement, not in the cash book.

The above procedure is illustrated in Table 3.4.2A on page 30.

TABLE 3.4.2A CLIENTS' CASH BOOK

Date	Cheque/C-Foil number	Client name	Narrative	Debit (Receipt) £	Credit (Payment) £	Balance £
			Balance b/fwd			13,000
5/1/95	642	Campbell Decd	Halifax B. Soc closure of A/C	10,000 ✓		23,000
8/1/95	114	Anderson	Stamp duty – Inland Revenue		1,200 ✓	21,800
10/1/95	115	Anderson	Estate agent's fees – Bloggs & Co		750 ✓	21,050
14/1/95	643	Baker	Payment on A/C of costs – of you	500 ✓		21,550
14/1/95	644	Martin	Receipt of damages – Insurance company	3,000 ✓		24,550
17/1/95	116	Jenkins	Local search – District Council		70 ✓	24,480
19/1/95	117	Reed	Medical report fee – Dr Brown		150 ✓	24,330
24/1/95	645	Jones	On account of disbursements	100 ✓		24,430
25/1/95	118	Roberts	Costs transfer		1,175 O/S	23,255
27/1/95	119	Jones	Local search – District Council		70 O/S	23,185
28/1/95	120	Evans	Stamp duty – Inland Revenue		800 O/S	22,385
31/1/95	646	Smith	Deposit – of you	2,000 O/S		24,385
			Closing cash book balance			24,385

✓ – cleared at bank in January
O/S – not yet presented

30

CLIENT ACCOUNT BANK STATEMENT NO. 42

Date 1995	Credit Number	Details	Debit (Payment)	Cheque (Receipt)	Balance
1 Jan		Balance			14,075
1 Jan		Bank Giro credit	O/S Dec	1,000✓	15,075
3 Jan	108		O/S Dec 500✓		14,575
5 Jan	110		O/S Dec 200✓		14,375
6 Jan		Bank Giro credit		10,000✓	24,375
12 Jan	115		750✓		23,625
13 Jan	109		O/S Dec 1,000✓		22,625
14 Jan	114		1,200✓		21,425
15 Jan		Bank Giro credit		3,500✓	24,925
20 Jan	117		150✓		24,775
21 Jan	116		70✓		24,705
25 Jan				100✓	24,805
27 Jan		Bank charges	Error 25		24,780

✓ = Agrees to January cash book

O/S Dec = Transaction appears in the firm's records in December.

Having identified any items that have not yet cleared through the bank, it is necessary to adjust the closing bank statement balance and prepare a bank reconciliation statement. When preparing the reconciliation statement it is important to use the actual bank statement figure at the date of the reconciliation. Thus, if the reconciliation is as at 31 January, take the bank statement balance at that date, otherwise the reconciliation will be overcomplicated.

Unpresented cheques should be listed chronologically to include the amount, the date that the cheque was written, and the cheque number. Cheques in excess of six months old are normally out of date and cannot be presented, although reference needs to be made to the firm's bankers for clarification of the position. Out-of-date cheques should be posted back to the books of account, investigated by the relevant fee earner and, where appropriate, cancelled and reissued.

There should be only a few outstanding lodgements or uncleared transfers, and these should be listed by reference to the amount and date, and should clear promptly in the following month. An outstanding lodgement appearing on more than one reconciliation statement will need to be investigated. Bank errors should be listed by reference to the amount and date, and on identification it is necessary to inform the bank immediately, and advisable to obtain written confirmation from them that they are responsible for the error.

A typical reconciliation statement would be as follows:

CLIENT ACCOUNT BANK RECONCILIATION STATEMENT JANUARY 1995

£

Bank balance per statement number 42			24,780	
Add uncleared lodgement			2,000	31/1/95
Less unpresented cheques				
111	18/12/94	200		
112	21/12/94	75		
113	23/12/94	100		
118	25/1/95	1,175		
119	27/1/95	70		
120	28/1/95	800		
			(2,420)	
Bank error 27/1/95			25	Corrected 2/2/95
Reconciled bank balance			**24,385**	

3.4.3 Clients' cash book reconciliation

A closing cash book balance should be calculated at least every five weeks and should be reconciled to the agreed bank balance and clients' matter balances of even date. The closing cash book balance will then form the opening cash book balance for the following month. With computer systems, the cash book balance will invariably be calculated automatically. A running balance may be maintained on manual systems (see illustration); otherwise it will need to be calculated as follows:

	£
Opening cash book balance (brought forward from previous month)	13,000
Plus receipts	15,600
Minus payments and transfers	(4,215)
Closing January 1995 cash book balance (carry forward to next month)	**24,385**

It is significant to note that the cash book balance should never vary from the total of the clients' balances. Any variation may indicate an error in the double entry system and should be investigated immediately.

The closing cash book balance may need to be adjusted for items included on the bank statement but not in the cash book (other than bank errors), which may be as a result of posting or other errors.

3.4.4 Clients' matter balances

A list of clients' matter balances will need to be extracted from the clients' ledgers at least every five weeks, and the total of these balances should be compared with the cash book balance. As a matter of good practice, the listing should periodically include clients' zero balances in order to identify those matters that need to be archived. Similarly, it is prudent to extract office balances as well as client balances in order to identify any office credit balances on clients' ledger accounts which may indicate that client's money is being improperly held in office account. Any office credit balances on clients' ledger accounts should be investigated and corrected.

A debit or overdrawn balance on a client's ledger account, where no funds are held for that client in client account, should not be deducted from the total of the client credit balances when calculating the liabilities to clients. Client debit balances that cannot be properly offset against related matters constitute a shortage on client account and should be disclosed as such on the reconciliation statement.

Set out below is an example of how the extracted balances could be listed:

CLIENTS' LEDGER BALANCES
31 JANUARY 1995

Client name	Client		Office	
	£	£	£	£
	DR	CR	DR	CR
Baker		500	–	
Cambell Dec'd		15,000	255	
Casson		3,500	100	
Jones		30	–	
Martin		3,000	60	
Pearson		1,500	–	
Reed		50	–	
Smith		2,000	70	
Taylor	1,195			
Totals	**1,195 DR**	**25,580 CR**		
Total liabilities to clients		**25,580 CR**		

3.4.5 Reconciliation summary

It is considered good practice to prepare a reconciliation summary showing the comparisons required by Rule 11(5) and the cause of any differences. In the current example, such a summary would appear as follows:

	£
Reconciled bank balance	24,385
Cash book balance	24,385
Total of the clients' ledger balances	25,580
Difference	1,195

The difference represents a debit balance on the Taylor ledger corrected by an office-to-client transfer in February 1995.

3.4.6 Reconciliation of separate designated accounts

The requirements of Rule 11(5) apply equally to client's money held in separate designated bank or building society accounts, and these therefore need to be included in the reconciliations. It is necessary to reconcile to the most up-to-date bank statements, and it is advisable for these to be obtained monthly, where possible, and for building society passbooks to be updated regularly. In any event, a statement should be obtained where there has been any movement on the account. It will usually only be necessary to extract the bank and building society balances at the relevant date from the bank statements and passbooks. Adjustments are not usually necessary for uncleared items, and should only be required in respect of unposted interest. The combined cash book balance will need to be calculated (as illustrated previously), and a list of balances will need to be extracted from the designated account client ledgers. A separate reconciliation summary can be prepared for designated accounts, or they may be included as part of the general client account reconciliation summary.

3.4.7 Additional points

The format of both computer and manual reconciliations may vary. This is acceptable provided that the comparisons required by Rule 11(5) are undertaken and recorded appropriately. When using a computer accounts system, it is essential to ensure that the reconciliation procedures are fully understood. As a matter of good practice, the reconciling figures produced by a computer reconciliation report should be checked and marked accordingly. These checks would include ensuring that the computer bank statement figure agrees to the actual bank statement figure and that the three balances are in agreement. A manual summary of a computer reconciliation is often helpful.

Reconciliation statements are an important accounting record and should be readily to hand. The use of a central reconciliation file, which will also assist in the regular review of the reconciliation statements by principals, is therefore recommended.

Although it is not a requirement of the Rules, it is also good practice to prepare and review office account reconciliations on a monthly basis (see para. 4.1.2).

3.5 Accounting for Deposit Interest

3.5.1 Requirements of Rule 20

Under the deposit interest provisions contained in Part III of the Rules, solicitors have, in effect, two options:

- place the client's money in a separate designated bank or building society deposit account and account for all of the interest earned; or

- leave the client's money on general client account, and account for a sum equivalent to the interest it would have earned had it been placed in a separate designated deposit account (although solicitors may choose to account for a sum in lieu of interest at a higher rate at their own discretion).

A separate designated account does not therefore have to be opened, but will avoid the necessity of calculating the interest due at a later date.

3.5.2 Calculating interest due on money held in general client account

There is no specific *de minimis* figure in relation to accounting for deposit interest on client's money held in general client account. The *de minimis* provisions are contained in Rule 21 and operate by way of a table (see below), which sets out minimum amounts and lengths of time for which client's money may be held before deposit interest becomes due. In addition, a reasonableness test will need to be applied where a solicitor holds more than £20,000 for less than one week, holds money continuously which varies significantly in amount, or holds sums of money intermittently. Therefore, even though deposit interest may not be payable on sums held in general client account by reference to the table, it may still be appropriate for interest to be paid.

No. of weeks	Minimum amount held (£)
8	1,000
4	2,000
2	10,000
1	20,000

As an alternative to the above, it is permissible to include in standard terms of business a provision that deposit interest of £20 or less will not be payable. Where, however, the interest received exceeds £20, the whole amount will be payable. Full contracting-out of the deposit interest provisions is possible only in exceptional circumstances; guidance on this and other deposit interest matters has been issued by the Law Society (see Appendix E), and detailed advice may be obtained from the Society's Professional Ethics Division. Where a firm offsets the deposit interest payable against costs, the amount of interest deducted should be shown clearly on the bill of costs.

GENERAL ACCOUNTING SYSTEMS

Some computer systems have a notional deposit facility which calculates, on an ongoing basis, the interest that would be payable on money held in general client account if it were held in a separate designated deposit account.

3.5.3 Tax consequences

In paying deposit interest, a solicitor will need to determine whether the sum in lieu of interest is paid gross or net of tax, and reference should be made to the table below:

Type of account	Payment of interest by bank or building society	Consequences
Designated – where subject to tax deduction	Net	Pay the interest net to the client, who receives a basic rate tax credit. No further tax deductions for UK residents (unless the solicitor is assessable as an agent).
Designated – where paid gross (client money generally)	Gross	Pay the interest gross to the client, who is assessable on the interest payment as gross income. No deduction of tax for non-UK residents (unless the solicitor is assessable as an agent).
Bank and building society general client account deposit – always paid gross (client money generally and stake money)	Gross	Pay the interest gross to the client who, in turn, is assessable on the interest payment as gross income. The solicitor will be assessed on the interest earned on general client account after setting off this payment to the client. No deduction of tax for non-UK residents.

3.5.4 Controlled trusts

Difficulties may arise where controlled trust money is held in general client account, as the deposit interest provisions do not apply to controlled trust money. Under the general law, a solicitor cannot benefit from his or her position as a trustee of a controlled trust. This effectively means that all interest earned on controlled trust money held in general client account, however small the sum held and for whatever length of time, must be accounted for at the rate at which it was actually received. In order to simplify administration, it is advisable to hold as much controlled trust money as possible in a controlled trust account for each individual controlled trust matter. Solicitors may also consider, subject to their duty to the trust, the use of a general non-interest bearing client account for controlled trust matters, thereby ensuring that they do not make an improper benefit from the trusts.

3.5.5 Compliance system

It is recommended that it should be the responsibility of each fee earner to ensure that any deposit interest payable is identified and paid to the client. Each client's ledger account should be reviewed by the fee earner on the conclusion of the matter in order to determine whether deposit interest is due. The Accounts Department will need to be advised accordingly and the necessary interest calculation undertaken, which will need to be confirmed by the fee earner, who should be responsible for authorising the payment. The necessary postings to both office and client account will then need to be made. Where separate designated deposit accounts are utilised, it is prudent for fee earners to review clients' matter balances regularly to identify instances where client's money needs to be placed in a separate designated deposit account.

3.6 ACCOUNTING FOR COMMISSION RECEIVED

3.6.1 Requirements of Solicitors' Practice Rule 10

Rule 10 of the Solicitors' Practice Rules 1990 requires that all commissions received by a solicitor in excess of £20 should be accounted for to the client unless the solicitor, having disclosed to the client in writing the amount or basis of calculation of the commission or (if the precise amount or basis cannot be ascertained) an approximation thereof, has the client's agreement to retain it.

Disclosure to the client must be in writing, and although it is not a requirement of the Practice Rule, it is preferable for the client's consent to also be in writing (it was made clear in the case of *Jordy* v. *Vanderpump* (1920) S.J. 324 that the onus is on the solicitor to prove the client's consent). Letters of commission disclosure and clients' authorities for the retention of commissions should be retained on a central file. Where the client has failed to consent to the retention of commission, the central file should contain evidence that the commission has been paid over to the client, preferably in the form of a signed receipt.

A solicitor may offset commission received against costs. The commission should, however, be clearly shown on the bill of costs and a copy of the bill retained on the central file.

Principals should ensure that all fee earners, particularly probate and trust staff, are aware of the requirements of Practice Rule 10, and that appropriate records of commissions received need to be maintained.

3.6.2 Accounting treatment of commission

The treatment of commissions received may be delegated to a member of the Accounts Department under the supervision of a principal. Where a commission cheque of less than £20 is received in respect of a client, this should be paid into office account. On receipt of a commission cheque in excess of £20 and an accompanying statement, the cashier should ascertain whether the client's consent to retention by the firm has been obtained, by reference to the central file. Where a client's consent has been obtained, the commission should be paid into the office account. If consent has not been obtained, the commission should be paid into client account and accounted for to the client.

Where a commission cheque is received that relates to a number of clients, and each respective commission is less than £20 or consent has been obtained from the relevant clients in respect of sums in excess of £20, the whole payment should be made into office account. If any part of the receipt includes commissions in excess of £20 and the corresponding clients have not given consent to retention by the firm, the whole receipt should be paid into client account. Any sums due to the firm should then be transferred to the office account as soon as possible, and the remaining money held on client account should be accounted for to the appropriate clients.

Under the Solicitors' Investment Business Rules 1995, which came into force on 1 June 1996, firms are required to keep a record of the total amount of commissions received which are attributable to investment business and the total amount of such commissions which are not paid or credited to clients (Rule 14, Solicitors' Investment Business Rules 1995).

Further information on the treatment of commissions is included in guidance that has been approved by the Law Society's Standards and Guidance Committee and is reproduced as Appendix F.

3.7 Clients' Files

It is important to maintain tidy, well-organised clients' files to aid ease of reference. The use of summary sheets recording key facts, events and documents during the course of a matter will assist when reviewing the file. For large or complicated matters, the use of separate files, e.g. correspondence file, documents file, tax or investment files, may be considered.

3.7.1 File closure and archiving procedure

Upon completion of a client's matter, certain checks should be undertaken before the file is closed and archived. Guidance on the retention/distribution of documents has been issued by the Law Society (see Appendix G). With regard to the accounts, the client's ledger account should be reviewed by the fee earner responsible for the matter, who should verify that:

(a) no deposit interest is due;

(b) there is a zero balance on client account;

(c) there is a zero balance on office account.

It should be noted that clients' balances, however small, should not simply be written off. Wherever possible, refunds should be made to the appropriate clients, but where clients cannot be traced, or the reasonable costs of doing so are likely to be excessively high in relation to the money held, balances may be transferred to a client miscellaneous or suspense ledger, provided the source of the funds is clearly identifiable and the original ledger is retained. Under Rule 8(2), an application for the release of such funds can then be made to the Law Society after a period of six years has elapsed. Guidance on this has been issued by the Society and is reproduced as Appendix D.

Ledgers relating to completed, archived matters should be retained by the Accounts Department on a central file and a copy kept with the corresponding client's file. Where a computer accounts system is used, it is recommended that hard copies of the client's ledger are printed off and retained in the same manner.

3.7.2 File retrieval system

Archived files should be stored securely, and clients' confidentiality should be preserved. Firms should implement an effective retrieval system to locate archived files. To assist with this, consideration could be given to colour-coding

GENERAL ACCOUNTING SYSTEMS

files according to work type, clear labelling and a number index system. If an archived file is removed from storage, a record of its removal should be maintained. Key documents, e.g. grants of probate, wills and deeds, should be stored separately, preferably in a fireproof facility. There are a number of matters to be considered before old files are destroyed, and guidance on these has been published by the Law Society (see Appendix G).

CHAPTER 4
Ensuring Compliance with the Rules

Some principals consider that once an accounting system and accounting procedures have been set up and a book-keeper employed to maintain the accounts, that is the end of their obligations, and the book-keeper can be left to deal with the accounts.

This section will now consider the ongoing responsibility for the maintenance and supervision of the books of account, the need for further training and development, and the implementation of safety controls.

4.1 THE PRINCIPALS OF THE FIRM

4.1.1 Responsibility

In a partnership, the responsibility for maintaining a proper book-keeping system is shared by all partners (including salaried partners). This is so even though the financial control of the firm may be delegated to one partner only. Any misappropriation or error by one partner is therefore the responsibility of all the partners. Moreover, all partners must ensure that any breaches of the Accounts Rules are remedied immediately. Of course, in sole practitioner firms, these responsibilities rest on the sole principal's shoulders alone.

Also, as a matter of conduct, a partner is prima facie responsible for the acts or omissions of the firm, and this extends to the acts or omissions of staff. Furthermore, as supported by Rule 13 of the Solicitors' Practice Rules 1990 (supervision and management), a solicitor is responsible for exercising proper supervision over both admitted and unadmitted staff, including not only employees but also independent contractors engaged to carry out work on behalf of the firm.

A sole principal and each of the principals in a partnership needs to be satisfied that fellow principals, other fee earners, employees and independent contractors alike are complying with the Solicitors' Accounts Rules (and, in a partnership, with the agreed financial control of the firm as a whole).

It is clear that even if, in a partnership, the financial control of the firm is delegated to one or more of the principals, the remaining principals remain equally liable. The remaining principals should still take an interest in the books of account and should, as frequently as they deem appropriate, check the books of account and satisfy themselves that these are being maintained properly.

The consequences of non-compliance with the Solicitors' Accounts Rules may be very costly and far reaching. Even if recourse can be made to the Solicitors' Indemnity Fund or Compensation Fund in the case of shortages of client money, the investigation and correction of any breaches of the Solicitors' Accounts Rules can be very time consuming and expensive. The additional services of the firm's accountant may be required to investigate fully and assist in the correction of any problems. Valuable fee-earning time may be spent reviewing client files and ledgers.

In a severe case, there may be further serious implications. While indemnity cover may be available, any claim will be subject to the payment by the principal(s) of the appropriate excess. In respect of a claim on the Compensation Fund, the Council may require the principal(s) to institute civil proceedings or to assist the police in connection with enquiries into the commission of any criminal offence in respect of any alleged acts giving rise to the claim.

If the Solicitors Complaints Bureau becomes involved, the matter may be referred to the Solicitors' Disciplinary Tribunal. The Tribunal has the power to make various orders: for example, in respect of the solicitor being struck off the Roll, his or her suspension from practice, the payment of a financial penalty and costs or a contribution to costs.

These are just a few of the consequences that could result from no, or poor, supervision of the accounts. Frequently, breaches of the Accounts Rules and problems arising on client matters can be identified when client account (and office account) reconciliations are considered.

4.1.2 Supervision

Principals should, of course, be familiar with both the current Accounts Rules and the firm's accounting systems. There are a number of ways in which principals may monitor the firm's compliance and also supervise the book-keeper effectively. It is strongly recommended, and considered to be a matter of good practice, that principals review the client account reconciliations: in what depth is left to their discretion. However, it should always be remembered that the principals of a firm remain ultimately liable for any breaches of the Solicitors' Accounts Rules and corresponding shortages of client money.

Paragraph 3.4 explains how a reconciliation should be prepared and how to interpret the reconciliation statement. Principals should understand the underlying purpose of the reconciliation and the manner in which the reconciliation is carried out. The reconciliation statement should confirm that sufficient client money is held overall to meet the firm's liabilities to clients. Principals should consider both the reconciliation statement, upon which the three balances that are compared are stated, and the accompanying list of client account (and office account) ledger balances.

A number of basic checks should be undertaken when reviewing client account reconciliations. The most fundamental test is to confirm that the clients' cash book balance agrees with the corresponding reconciled bank balance figure and the total of the clients' balances. The reconciliation statements should also be checked for unusual or recurring items. Adjustments should not be carried forward from month to month and outstanding lodgements should clear early in the following month. It is also wise to check that the correct figures have been taken from the client account bank and building society statements and passbooks.

With regard to ledger balances, an explanation should be sought in respect of any debit balances recorded on clients' ledger accounts. Office credit balances, old or large client balances and suspense ledger accounts should be queried and investigated by reference to the ledger accounts and clients' files where necessary.

There are a number of other reports that principals may also consider. Some sophisticated computer accounting systems allow 'exception' reports to be prepared: for example, reports that list any debit balances appearing on the client account columns or list any credit balances arising on the office account columns.

In addition, important management information may be obtained by considering, for example, office account reconciliations, reports listing bills delivered per fee earner or per department, or reports listing unpaid bills or new work per fee earner/department.

Considering financial reports relating to individual fee earners' client matters will assist principals in meeting their responsibility to supervise fee earners. With a manual accounting system, the financial reports available may be limited. However, with both computer and manual accounting systems, consideration can be given to client and office account balances extracted from the client ledgers, and bills delivered relating to each fee earner's matters.

This guide is primarily concerned with compliance with the Solicitors' Accounts Rules and, therefore, client and office account transactions relating to client matters. However, some comment must be made on the management of the firm as a whole.

Whether a manual or a computer accounting system is used, it is essential that principals monitor cash flow and the profitability of their firms in order to be able to plan and budget for the future. The firm's books of account should be capable of providing this information. Although not a requirement of the Accounts Rules, it is considered to be good practice for office account reconciliations to be carried out at least as frequently as client account reconciliations. Principals should be able to monitor the firm's fee income and credit control and relate these to fee earners and work types, with regular checks and assessment of this information being carried out. The principals should request and consider sufficient information to monitor the firm's financial standing and viability not just yearly, but at regular intervals throughout the year.

4.2 The Book-keeper

Most firms employ one or more full-time or part-time book-keepers. Some firms use a self-employed book-keeper or independent book-keeping firm or even an employee of the firm's accountant. Some principals may have the required competence to maintain the books of account themselves, but should consider very carefully whether this will be feasible in addition to dealing with their own client workload. If problems start to develop then assistance should be obtained immediately or the situation will only worsen.

The book-keeper must be competent, reliable and fully conversant with the Solicitors' Accounts Rules. Previous experience in maintaining solicitors' books of account is preferable, and a recognised book-keeping or accountancy qualification is an asset. If the book-keeper does not have a relevant qualification, he or she should have appropriate previous experience; remember that solicitors' accounts differ significantly from accounts that are maintained for other professions or industry. In deciding who is to maintain the firm's books of account, the principal may decide to seek the assistance of the firm's accountant.

Principals must ascertain the extent of a prospective book-keeper's knowledge and experience. Has the book-keeper previous knowledge or experience of a computer or manual accounting system: in particular, the one used by the firm? Will the book-keeper be able to deal with all the various accounting functions? Has the book-keeper dealt with the accounts arising from the areas of work covered by the firm? Can he or she provide references?

The Solicitors' Accounts Rules require the books of account to be properly written up 'at all times' [Rule 11(1)]. In small firms it is recommended that the books of account are written up at least weekly, and daily in larger firms. Care should be taken to ensure that the book-keeper is in a position to comply with this recommendation.

While the book-keeper may be competent, this does not discharge the principals' obligation to supervise the book-keeper, or the principals' duty to ensure that the books of account are maintained properly and kept up to date.

Regular communication with the book-keeper is important. The supervising principal(s) should cultivate a good working relationship with the book-keeper so that he or she freely and readily reports to and consults with the principal(s) in question. It is probably wise, in view of the ever-present pressure of work, to set aside a regular meeting time, perhaps weekly, but at the very least five-weekly when the client account (and, hopefully, office account) reconciliations are conducted.

4.3 THE REPORTING ACCOUNTANT

Every solicitor who holds or receives client's money or money subject to a controlled trust must produce an annual report under section 34 of the Solicitors Act 1974. The Accountant's Report Rules 1991 explain how this must be done (see Appendix C).

Principals need to decide what further services they wish the reporting accountant to provide; the accountant's terms of reference should be agreed and understood fully. For example, is the accountant simply required to do sufficient to enable him or her to prepare the annual report for the Law Society, or is he or she required to conduct a full audit of both office and client account, prepare cash flow forecasts, provide tax advice and support, etc.? All concerned need to know what will be undertaken in return for the accountant's fees.

It can be useful to employ a local accountant. This chapter includes many references to ways in which the accountant can assist the principals by providing advice and guidance that will help them meet their responsibility to maintain up-to-date and accurate books of account.

4.4 Fee Earners and Staff

Fee earners should possess a good understanding of the Solicitors' Accounts Rules and the firm's internal accounting procedures to enable them to deal properly with financial transactions relating to matters that they are handling.

Steps should be taken to ensure that fee earners and staff understand the firm's manual records or computer print-outs of client ledgers and any other reports that they are asked to consider and check. Fee earners should be encouraged to undertake regular reviews of their own client matters: for example, by viewing lists of office and client account balances relating to matters that they are dealing with.

Fee earners and staff should have a point of reference if they have queries regarding the accounts or the firm's accounting procedures, perhaps an office manual and/or a member of staff in the Accounts Department. It is important that they are given the opportunity to discuss any queries regarding the books of account with the book-keeper or supervising principal(s).

Fee earners and staff also need to be made aware of any changes in the Accounts Rules or internal accounting procedures, and checks should be made to ensure that such changes are clearly understood and have been adopted. The book-keeper will be able to maintain accurate and up-to-date books of account only if internal accounting procedures are followed and prompt replies are given to matters raised by him or her.

4.5 Training and Development

4.5.1 Changes to the Solicitors' Accounts Rules

The Guide to the Professional Conduct of Solicitors 1996, published by the Law Society and updated by the Professional Standards Bulletins Numbers 16 onwards (which are issued by the Professional Ethics Division of the Law Society to all solicitors holding a current practising certificate), contains *inter alia* the up-to-date Solicitors' Accounts Rules. The Guide and the Bulletins also contain very useful guidance and further information regarding issues concerning these Rules.

Arrangements should be made to ensure that the book-keeper, principals, fee earners and staff have available and understand the current Rules and are made aware of any changes.

Training and development of the book-keeper is of equal importance as that for other fee earners. Courses, both short and long term, perhaps leading to book-keeping qualifications, are organised throughout the country, and many accountancy organisations produce their own professional journal containing useful information. Remember, it may not just be changes in the Accounts Rules that the book-keeper needs to be made aware of and absorb but also changes to matters such as tax, National Insurance and VAT.

It may be that the firm's accountant could also assist in ensuring that the book-keeper is kept abreast of any developments that will affect his or her work. Guidance on the Solicitors' Accounts Rules and associated controls can also be sought from the Professional Ethics Division.

4.5.2 Changes within the firm

Principals should remember that any changes in the areas of work dealt with by the firm may have repercussions in the Accounts Department. For example, the book-keeper may be experienced in dealing with financial transactions emanating from private client matters, but may need additional training to adapt to dealing with legally aided matters, or vice versa.

A change in work types covered by the firm may also require a change in accounting procedures within the firm, and necessitate the establishment of new arrangements with external organisations. The book-keeper should work closely with the principals to agree upon and implement such new systems. The Accounts Rules should be considered to ensure that any proposed new accounting systems and procedures meet the requirements set out in those Rules. For example, many banks now offer an electronic terminal link that can be installed at the firm's offices to enable transfers between the client and office accounts to be processed by the firm itself, and even allows the firm to transmit funds from its own bank accounts. If a firm proposes to use such a terminal, checks should be made to ensure that Rules 4, 7, 8, 11(6) and 11(9) are complied with.

New systems should be communicated to the rest of the firm, perhaps with a guidance note, and, if appropriate, corresponding training should be provided.

4.5.3 Changes in book-keeping staff

There may, of course, be changes of personnel within the Accounts Department from time to time. Enough time should be set aside for new personnel to be given training on the accounting systems employed by the firm and the accounting procedures used.

If there is a complete change of the personnel responsible for the day-to-day maintenance of the books of account, close supervision is required to ensure that the take-over is smooth and any initial problems are sorted out quickly. It is essential to have an early review as well as ongoing reviews of new staff's work. The longer problems are allowed to exist, the more difficult and time-consuming it will be to rectify them.

4.5.4 Changes in the book-keeping system used

If a change in the actual book-keeping system used takes place, training will be essential. It is wrong to assume that because, for example, the firm is changing from one computer accounting system to another the book-keeper will adapt easily. To decide not to incur the additional expense of training on a new computer system will be a false economy. Given adequate training, the book-keeper will adapt far more quickly, and it is more likely that the new system will be used properly and to its full potential.

It may be possible to negotiate as part of the contract with the computer software supplier that every time the company modifies that particular system, whether due to Rule changes or general improvements, the firm's system will also be updated. Further training of the book-keeping staff at that point would again be wise. In addition, it is useful if the company supplying the computer software operates a 'helpline' or can put the firm in touch with other users of the same system.

It is essential that sufficient time is provided for the book-keeper to adapt to a new system and to bring forward the accounts information from the old system, as well as dealing with ongoing day-to-day transactions and accounting functions. The software supplier and/or the firm's accountant may assist in introducing the accounts information onto the new system.

It is recommended that the firm continues to maintain the old accounting system as a back-up until all are confident that the new accounting system is working properly. Again, an early review of the progress made in using the new accounting system with the computer software supplier and/or the firm's accountant is sensible.

It is important to consider all these points before embarking on a change in the accounting system used. Not only does a change in accounting system need proper planning and consideration as to how it will be achieved and how it will affect the firm as a whole, but the principals will need to consider all such salient points in assessing the true cost, in terms both of time and expenditure, that a change in the firm's accounting system will entail.

It is not proposed that this guide should deal with how to select an accounting system; there are a number of sources of information to assist in the selection. Many software suppliers are willing to visit a firm and demonstrate their systems, and also attend exhibitions with other suppliers throughout the year.

The firm's accountant may also assist and may in fact employ a consultant, or be able to recommend a consultant, who can assist the firm in the selection of an accounting system that meets its specific needs and requirements. The firm's accounts staff should also be consulted for their views on a prospective system.

The Law Society's Practice Advice Service (telephone 0171 242 1222) can answer general enquiries about practice management, including those about information technology and the Practice Management Standards. The Practice Advice Service are also able to supply guidelines and factsheets about the use of legal accounting software.

4.6 Internal Security and Controls

Security within the Accounts Department should be considered. Again, principals must take their responsibilities seriously, and each system whereby money is controlled or handled should be examined from the point of view of security.

4.6.1 Responsibility

As detailed at the start of this chapter, every principal of a firm is responsible for ensuring that the firm's books of account are up to date and maintained in compliance with the Solicitors' Accounts Rules. They should ensure that any breaches of these Rules are rectified immediately on discovery. If breaches result in a shortage of client money, the principals are under an obligation to replace the monies immediately.

Principals also have a duty to safeguard client's money, and should ensure that effective safeguards and controls are built into the firm's accounting systems and procedures so that they are not open to abuse by persons from within the firm as well as from outside.

Proper supervision of the book-keeper and the maintenance of the books of account is crucial. Controls and precautionary systems can be implemented to help prevent client money being misappropriated and to preserve the books of account.

Remember that even hitherto responsible and trustworthy employees may succumb to temptation if the firm's systems are lax and offer potential for abuse.

4.6.2 Receipt of money

How safe is incoming money, whether it is received in the post or directly from a client?

As explained in para. 3.1.1, it is good practice for the opening of post to be supervised by a principal, and each item can be marked to record whether it was accompanied by a cheque or cash. Some firms maintain a book that records such incoming mail each day, and which can be compared with the paying-in book and/or bank statements. Thought needs to be given to the safe keeping of money pending its being banked. A receipt should be given to a client if cash is provided, and a copy of the receipt should be retained on the client's file.

Does the same person who completes the paying-in book also physically do the banking? Is this the same person that maintains the books of account? If the answer is 'yes' to these questions then an opportunity for abuse may exist. Principals should consider how easy it would be for this person to steal client money and cover their tracks, and what procedures could be implemented to prevent such an opportunity arising.

4.6.3 Withdrawal of money

The procedures for withdrawing money from the firm's bank and building society accounts should also be considered. As far as client accounts are concerned, Rule 11(6) sets out certain categories of people who are entitled to sign authorities for the withdrawal of money. Client accounts include general client accounts and separate designated accounts, whether at banks or at building societies. All withdrawals are covered, whether made by means of a cheque, telegraphic transfer, direct transfer, etc.

The mandate for the bank and building society accounts should provide for persons falling within the categories set out in Rule 11(6) to operate the accounts. The firm may also consider arranging for an additional signatory to sign cheques jointly with someone entitled under Rule 11(6). For example, if a solicitor, holding a current practising certificate, not being a principal of the firm, is permitted to sign withdrawal authorities (in accordance with Rule 11(6)), the principals may consider that this should only be on the basis that, as a precaution, the book-keeper also signs the authority.

The bank or building society should be checking that any withdrawal authorities are signed pursuant to the provisions of the mandate or signatory card for the account. However, if the paid cheques are returned by the bank, it is recommended that a principal and/or the book-keeper checks that they have been signed pursuant to the mandate or signatory card, and have not been forged or tampered with in any way.

It is also considered safer to direct that those persons signing withdrawal authorities sign using their personal signatures rather than signing in the firm's name, as the former are likely to be harder to forge.

Similarly, it is also strongly recommended that in order to safeguard client's money against misappropriation when writing out a cheque in favour of a bank or building society, after the payee's name should be added the account name or account number into which the cheque is to be placed. For example, if drawing a cheque for the redemption of a building society mortgage, the mortgage roll number could be added after the building society's name.

Cheques, transfers or other withdrawal authorities should be accompanied by relevant documentation such as letters, forms and completion statements, so that the person(s) signing them can check their bona fides. The book-keeper should check that sufficient funds are held for a client before a payment out can be processed, and should be instructed to refuse to process a withdrawal from a client account if it will create a debit balance on the client account columns of a client ledger, or a transfer to (or direct payment into) the office account if it will produce a credit balance on the office columns of a client ledger.

A signatory should be extra vigilant when signing cheques to cash, and should seek an explanation as to why a payment to cash is required. A cheque payable to cash should not be sent by post; it is recommended that the client should be required to attend the office personally and, if possible, should be accompanied to the bank.

The firm's system for arranging for telegraphic transfers should be examined carefully to establish whether unauthorised withdrawals could be made. Rule 11(6) requires a signed authority to be in place before a withdrawal from a client account is actually made. Some banks will accept instructions by telephone to send money by telegraphic transfer. At the time that the telephone instruction is given, the signed authority must be in existence but may not actually have been received by the bank when the bank withdraws the money from the client account. Additional safeguards are therefore required. For example, the bank and the principal(s) may agree to use a list of passwords or codes, which should preferably be kept safely by the principal(s). Every time a telegraphic transfer takes place, the appropriate principal can communicate the next password or code on the list to the book-keeper, who can quote it to the bank when the instruction is given. Alternatively, the principal can add the code or password to the withdrawal authority that he or she signs and the bank can be instructed not to process the telegraphic transfer until this has been received via facsimile transmission or delivered by hand.

Another safeguard would be to arrange for the bank to call the firm back and confirm the telephone instruction (or written instruction) with someone within the firm other than the person who gave the instruction.

Whichever system is used, it is far safer to arrange with the bank that the telegraphic transfer will not be processed until the written authority has been received from the firm signed pursuant to the bank mandate and with any password or code endorsed. This will provide for another check on the bona fides of the instruction.

4.6.4 Safe keeping of other accounting material

Unused cheque books, telegraphic transfer forms, building society passbooks, etc., should be kept somewhere safe, preferably under lock and key. They should not be allowed to circulate freely around the office.

Special attention needs to be paid to the safe keeping of passbooks, cheque books and paying-in books (if applicable) in relation to separate designated accounts. It is preferable for such passbooks to be kept centrally by the book-keeper (in a safe or other secure place) rather than on individual client files. Any transactions on the accounts will then of necessity involve the Accounts Department, and will ensure that the transactions are entered promptly in the books of account.

4.6.5 Organisation of the Accounts Department

The organisation of the Accounts Department can be considered both from the point of view of safeguarding client (and office) money and from the point of view having back-up systems in case of unforeseen problems.

If the Accounts Department is run by one person alone, then the principals should consider what cover is available in the event of planned and unforeseen absences of the book-keeper from the office. Appropriate cover should be in place, ready to minimise any disruption that such absences may cause.

Steps need to be taken to ensure that the book-keeper is not the only person who can operate the firm's computer accounting system. On the other hand, if several people have access to the computer, care should be taken to limit their rights of access to either view-only or to their specific accounting functions.

Where accounting duties are split between employees, it is worth considering operating a rota system so that, for example, the same person is not always responsible for completing the paying-in book and physically banking money. Spot checks of each employee's work could also be carried out. In addition, the access of other employees and fee earners to the Accounts Department itself could be limited.

Principals should also consider how the firm would fare if the books of account were destroyed or a fault developed on the firm's computer accounting system. Consideration should be given to the records that the firm retains which would allow the books of account to be reconstructed without recourse to perusing each individual client file. Back-up procedures should be determined: for example, daily and/or monthly security discs can be used. Manual accounting systems can be protected by being stored in a fireproof box.

4.6.6 Fraud prevention

The Accounts Department has an important role to play in assisting the principal in identifying potentially problematic transactions. Solicitors should now be fully aware of the risk of being involved or implicated in a mortgage fraud. The book-keeper, together with all other staff, should be encouraged to watch out for signs of mortgage fraud and report any concerns to the principals immediately. The book-keeper should be made aware of the Warning Card on property fraud issued by the Law Society (see Appendix I), or perhaps a checklist of points to look out for could be prepared for the book-keeper to refer to. Principals should be mindful

ENSURING COMPLIANCE WITH THE RULES

that failure to observe signs of mortgage fraud, such as those listed in the Warning Card, and to take appropriate steps, may be taken into account if any civil or criminal proceedings were to follow.

The Law Society has also issued a Warning Card in relation to the Money Laundering Regulations 1993 and the Criminal Justice Act 1993 (see Appendix H). If solicitors do not take steps to become acquainted with these provisions, and fail to implement appropriate safeguards, they may commit a criminal offence by assisting someone known or suspected to be laundering money generated by serious crime, by telling clients or anyone else that they are under investigation for an offence of money laundering, or by failing to report a suspicion of money laundering in the case of drug trafficking or terrorism (unless certain exceptions apply). Additionally, solicitors who engage in investment business within the meaning of the Financial Services Act 1986 must take steps to comply with the Regulations. Again, the book-keeper should be encouraged to assist in identifying potential money laundering transactions, and to report these to the firm's nominated money laundering reporting officer.

Solicitors are also vulnerable to fraudsters who may attempt to involve them and/or their clients in other financial scams. A warning has already been issued to all solicitors about such scams (see Appendix J).

The book-keeper should be encouraged to report any suspect transaction to a principal for verification or investigation. For example:

- large cash transactions;
- transactions that do not follow the usual format – for example, a conveyancing transaction that does not involve the payment of a deposit, or where the deposit is paid direct;
- transactions involving the same client obtaining a number of mortgages over different properties, or where the client is buying a number of properties from different people, all of whom are using the same solicitor;
- transactions that have simply involved the firm holding large sums of money;
- transactions involving foreign currency or foreign banks, particularly where the country is known for drug production or trafficking.

If a principal is concerned as to the bona fides of a proposed transaction then he or she should seek guidance. The Professional Ethics Division of the Law Society (telephone 0171 242 1222 or 01527 517141) will provide guidance, and will deal with any queries on a confidential and, if required, anonymous basis. Any concerns that a firm may have can be brought to the attention of the Law Society's Fraud Intelligence Officer (who is based in the Monitoring Unit at Redditch – direct line: 0171 320 5703) or can be reported via the Solicitors Complaints Bureau's 'Red Alert' hotline (telephone 01926 431671). The local Law Society may also be consulted and, indeed, may have been contacted by other firms that have been approached by the same prospective fraudster.

APPENDIX A
Solicitors' Accounts Rules 1991

(WITH CONSOLIDATED AMENDMENTS TO 1 JUNE 1992)

Rules dated 16 July 1991 made by the Council of the Law Society and approved by the Master of the Rolls pursuant to section 32 of the Solicitors Act 1974 and section 9 of the Administration of Justice Act 1985 regulating the keeping of accounts by solicitors, registered foreign lawyers and recognised bodies in respect of their English and Welsh practices.

Commencement and interpretation

1. These rules may be cited as the Solicitors' Accounts Rules 1991 and shall come into operation on the 1st day of June 1992 whereupon the Solicitors' Accounts Rules 1986, the Solicitors' Trust Accounts Rules 1986 and the Solicitors' Accounts (Deposit Interest) Rules 1988 shall cease to have effect.

2. (1) In these Rules, unless the context otherwise requires–

   the expressions "accounts", "books", "ledgers" and "records" shall be deemed to include loose-leaf books and such cards or other permanent documents or records as are necessary for the operation of any system of book-keeping, computerised, mechanical or otherwise and where a computerised system is operated, the information recorded on it must be capable of being reproduced in hard printed form within a reasonable time;

   "bank" shall mean the branch, situated in England or Wales, of a bank as defined by section 87(1) of the Solicitors Act 1974, as amended by paragraph 9 of Schedule 6 to the Banking Act 1979 and paragraph 5 of Schedule 6 to the Banking Act 1987;

   "building society" shall mean the branch, situated in England or Wales, of a building society as defined by paragraph 11(5) of Schedule 18 to the Building Societies Act 1986;

"client", save in Part III of these rules, shall mean any person on whose account a solicitor holds or receives client's money;

"client account" shall mean a current or deposit account at a bank or deposit account with a building society in the name of the solicitor or his or her firm in the title of which account the word "client" appears;

"client's money" shall mean money held or received by a solicitor on account of a person for whom he or she is acting in relation to the holding or receipt of such money either as a solicitor or, in connection with his or her practice as a solicitor, as agent, bailee, stakeholder or in any other capacity; provided that the expression "client's money" shall not include–

(a) money held or received on account of the trustees of a trust of which the solicitor is a controlled trustee; or

(b) money to which the only person entitled is the solicitor himself or herself or, in the case of a firm of solicitors, one or more of the partners in the firm;

"controlled trust" in relation to a solicitor, shall mean a trust of which he or she is a controlled trustee;

"controlled trust account" shall mean a current or deposit account kept at a bank or deposit account kept with a building society in the title of which the word "trustee" or "executor" appears, or which is otherwise clearly designated as a controlled trust account, and kept solely for money subject to a particular trust of which the solicitor is a controlled trustee;

"controlled trustee" shall mean a solicitor who is a sole trustee or co-trustee only with one or more of his or her partners or employees and any reference to a controlled trustee shall be construed as including–

(a) a recognised body which is a sole trustee or co-trustee only with one or more of its officers, partners or employees; and

(b) a solicitor or a recognised body who or which is an officer or employee of a recognised body and who or which is a sole trustee or co-trustee only with one or more other officers or employees of that recognised body or the body itself;

"costs" includes fees, charges, disbursements, expenses and remuneration and, for the purpose of rules 7(a)(iv) and 9(2)(c)(i), shall include costs (including VAT) in respect of which a solicitor has incurred a liability but shall exclude the fees of counsel or other lawyer, or of a professional or other agent, or of an expert instructed by the solicitor;

"local authority" shall have the same meaning as is given to this expression by the Local Government Act 1972;

"private loan" shall mean a loan other than one provided by an institution which provides loans in the normal course of its activities;

"public officer" shall mean an officer whose remuneration is defrayed out of moneys provided by Parliament, the revenues of the Duchy of Cornwall or the Duchy of Lancaster, the general fund of the Church Commissioners, the Forestry Fund or the Development Fund;

"recognised body" shall have the meaning assigned to it by the Solicitors' Incorporated Practice Rules 1988 as may be amended, modified or re-enacted from time to time;

"separate designated account" shall mean a deposit account at a bank or building society in the name of the solicitor or his or her firm in the title of which account the word "client" appears and which is designated by reference to the identity of the client or matter concerned;

"solicitor" shall mean a solicitor of the Supreme Court and shall include a firm of solicitors or a recognised body;

"statutory undertakers" shall mean any person authorised by or under an Act of Parliament, to construct, work, or carry on any railway, canal, inland navigation, dock, harbour, tramway, gas, electricity, water or other public undertaking;

"trust money" shall mean money held or received by a solicitor which is not client's money and which is subject to a trust of which the solicitor is a trustee whether or not he or she is a controlled trustee of such trust;

words in the singular include the plural, words in the plural include the singular and words importing the masculine or feminine shall include the neuter; and

(2) Other expressions in these rules shall except where otherwise stated have the meanings assigned to them by the Solicitors Act 1974.

Part I – General

3. Subject to the provisions of rule 9 hereof, every solicitor who holds or receives client's money, or money which under rule 4 hereof the solicitor is permitted and elects to pay into a client account, shall without delay pay such money into a client account. Any solicitor may keep one client account or as many such accounts as the solicitor thinks fit.

4. There may be paid into a client account–

    (a) trust money;

    (b) such money belonging to the solicitor as may be necessary for the purpose of opening or maintaining the account;

    (c) money to replace any sum which for any reason may have been drawn from the account in contravention of paragraph (2) of rule 8 of these rules; and

    (d) money received by the solicitor which under paragraph (b) of rule 5 of these rules the solicitor is entitled to split but which the solicitor does not split.

5. Where a solicitor holds or receives money which includes client's money or trust money of one or more trusts–

    (a) he or she may where practicable split such money and, if he or she does so, he or she shall deal with each part thereof as if he or she had received a separate sum of money in respect of that part; or

    (b) if he or she does not split the money he or she shall, if any part thereof consists of client's money, and may, in any other case, pay the money into a client account.

5A. When a solicitor receives, in full or part settlement of a bill of costs, a payment all of which is money to which the solicitor alone is entitled, the solicitor may, as an alternative to treating the money in accordance with rule 9(2), elect to pay it without delay into a client account *provided that* the money does not remain in a client account longer than seven days from receipt.

6. No money other than money which under the foregoing rules a solicitor is required or permitted to pay into a client account shall be paid into a client account, and it shall be the duty of a solicitor into whose client account any money has been paid in contravention of this rule to withdraw the same without delay on discovery.

APPENDIX A: SOLICITORS' ACCOUNTS RULES 1991

7. There may be drawn from a client account–

   (a) in the case of client's money–

   (i) money properly required for a payment to or on behalf of the client;

   (ii) money properly required in full or partial reimbursement of money expended by the solicitor on behalf of the client;

   (iii) money drawn on the client's authority;

   (iv) money properly required for or towards payment of the solicitor's costs where there has been delivered to the client a bill of costs or other written intimation of the amount of the costs incurred and it has thereby or otherwise in writing been made clear to the client that money held for him or her is being or will be applied towards or in satisfaction of such costs; and

   (v) money which is transferred into another client account;

   (b) in the case of trust money–

   (i) money properly required for a payment in the execution of the particular trust, and

   (ii) money to be transferred to a separate bank or building society account kept solely for the money of the particular trust;

   (c) money, not being money to which either paragraph (a) or paragraph (b) of this rule applies, as may have been paid into the account under rule 4(b) or rule 5(b) or rule 5A of these rules;

   (d) money which for any reason may have been paid into the account in contravention of rule 6 of these rules;

   provided that in any case under paragraph (a) and paragraph (b) of this rule the money so drawn shall not exceed the total of the money held for the time being in such account on account of such client or trust.

8. (1) No money drawn from a client account under sub-paragraph (ii) or sub-paragraph (iv) of paragraph (a) or under paragraph (c) or paragraph (d) of rule 7 of these rules shall be drawn except by–

   (a) a cheque drawn in favour of the solicitor, or

   (b) a transfer to a bank or building society account in the name of the solicitor not being a client account.

61

COMPLYING WITH THE SOLICITORS' ACCOUNTS RULES: A PRACTICAL GUIDE

(2) No money other than money permitted by rule 7 to be drawn from a client account shall be so drawn unless the Council upon an application made to them by the solicitor specifically authorise in writing its withdrawal.

9. (1) Notwithstanding the provisions of these rules, a solicitor shall not be under an obligation to pay into a client account client's money held or received by him or her—

(a) which is received by him or her in the form of cash and is without delay paid in cash in the ordinary course of business to the client or on his or her behalf to a third party; or

(b) which is received by him or her in the form of a cheque or draft which is endorsed over in the ordinary course of business to the client or on his or her behalf to a third party and is not passed by the solicitor through a bank or building society account; or

(c) which he or she pays into a separate bank or building society account opened or to be opened in the name of the client or of some person designated by the client in writing or acknowledged by the solicitor to the client in writing.

(2) Notwithstanding the provisions of these rules (and except where the solicitor elects to treat a payment in accordance with rule 5A and complies with the requirements of that rule), a solicitor shall not pay into a client account money held or received by him or her—

(a) which the client for his or her own convenience requests the solicitor to withhold from such account, such request being either in writing from the client or acknowledged by the solicitor to the client in writing; or

(b) which is received by him or her from the client in full or partial reimbursement of money expended by the solicitor on behalf of the client; or

(c) which is expressly paid to him or her either—

(i) for or towards payment of the solicitor's costs in respect of which a bill of costs or other written intimation of the amount of the costs incurred has been delivered for payment; or

(ii) as an agreed fee (or on account of an agreed fee) for business undertaken or to be undertaken.

(3) Where money includes client's money as well as money of the nature described in paragraph (2) of this rule such money shall be dealt with in accordance with rule 5 of these rules.

(4) Notwithstanding the provisions of these rules the Council may upon application made to them by a solicitor specifically authorise such solicitor in writing to withhold any client's money from a client account.

10. (1) No sum shall be transferred from the ledger account of one client to that of another except in circumstances in which it would have been permissible under these rules to have withdrawn from client account the sum transferred from the first client and to have paid into client account the sum so transferred to the second client.

(2) No sum in respect of a private loan shall be paid–

(a) directly; or

(b) by means of a transfer from the ledger account of one client to that of another;

out of funds held on account of the lender without the prior written authority of the lender.

11. (1) Every solicitor shall at all times keep properly written up such accounts as may be necessary–

(a) to show the solicitor's dealings with–

(i) client's money received, held or paid by him or her; and

(ii) any other money dealt with by him or her through a client account; and

(b) (i) subject to rule 11 (3) below to show separately in respect of each client all money of the categories specified in sub-paragraph (a) of this paragraph which is received, held or paid by him or her on account of that client; and

(ii) to distinguish all money of the said categories received, held or paid by him or her, from any other money received, held or paid by him or her; and

(c) to show the current balance on each client's ledger.

(2) (a) All dealings referred to in sub-paragraph (a) of paragraph (1) of this rule shall be appropriately recorded–

    (i) in a clients' cash account; or a clients' column of a cash account or in a record of sums transferred from the ledger account of one client to that of another; and

    (ii) in a clients' ledger or a clients' column of a ledger; and no other dealings shall be recorded in such clients' cash account, ledger, record of sums transferred or, as the case may be, in such clients' columns.

(b) All dealings of the solicitor relating to his or her practice as a solicitor other than those referred to in sub-paragraph (a) of paragraph (1) of this rule shall (subject to compliance with Part II of these rules) be recorded in a separate cash account and ledger or such other columns of a cash account and ledger as the solicitor may maintain.

(3) A solicitor acting for both borrower and lender in a conveyancing transaction who receives from the lender a mortgage advance shall not be required to open separate ledger accounts for both borrower and lender in respect of such advance provided that–

(a) the funds belonging to each client are clearly identifiable; and

(b) the lender is an institutional lender which provides mortgages in the normal course of its activities.

(4) In addition to the books, ledgers and records referred to in paragraph (2) of this rule, every solicitor shall keep a record of all bills of costs (distinguishing between profit costs and disbursements) and of all written intimations under rule 7(a)(iv) and under rule 9(2)(c) of these rules delivered or made by the solicitor to his or her clients, which record shall be contained in a bills delivered book or a file of copies of such bills and intimations.

(5) Every solicitor shall, at least once every five weeks–

(i) compare the total of the balances shown by the clients' ledger accounts of the liabilities to the clients, including those for whom trust money is held in the client account, with the cash account balance; and

(ii) prepare a reconciliation statement showing the cause of the difference, if any, shown by the above comparison; and

APPENDIX A: SOLICITORS' ACCOUNTS RULES 1991

    (iii)   reconcile that cash account balance with the balances shown on client account bank and building society pass books or statements and money held elsewhere;

and shall preserve the records of all such reconciliations.

(6)   A withdrawal from a bank or building society account, being or forming part of a client account, may only be made where a specific authority in respect of that withdrawal has been signed by one at least of the following (either alone or in conjunction with other persons) namely–

    (i)   a solicitor who holds a current practising certificate; or

    (ii)   an employee of such a solicitor being either a solicitor or a Fellow of the Institute of Legal Executives who is confirmed by the Institute as being of good standing and who shall have been admitted a Fellow for not less than three years;

    (iia)   a registered foreign lawyer who is a partner or director of the practice;

    (iii)   in the case of an office dealing solely with conveyancing, an employee of such a solicitor being a licensed conveyancer.

(7)   Rule 11(6) shall not apply to the transfer of money from one account to another at the same bank or building society where both accounts are client accounts other than separate designated accounts.

(8)   For the purposes of rule 11 (6) of these rules the first and third references to a solicitor shall not be construed as including references to a recognised body and the references to an employee of 'such a solicitor' shall be construed as including a reference to an employee of a recognised body.

(9)   (a)   Every solicitor shall preserve for at least six years–

        (i)   from the date of the last entry therein all accounts, books, ledgers and records; and

        (ii)   all bank statements as printed and issued by the bank.

    (b)   Every solicitor shall retain for at least two years-

        (i)   all paid cheques unless he or she has arranged in writing with the relevant bank(s) and/or building society(ies) that they will retain such paid cheques for that period; and

(ii) copies of the authorities (other than cheques) signed pursuant to rule 11(6).

(10) This rule 11 shall apply only to Part I of these rules.

Part II – Controlled Trusts

12. Subject to the provisions of rule 18 of these rules every controlled trustee who holds or receives money subject to a trust of which he or she is a controlled trustee, other than money which is paid into a client account as permitted by Part I of these rules, shall without delay pay such money into a controlled trust account of the particular trust.

13. There may be paid into a controlled trust account–

    (a) money subject to the particular trust;

    (b) such money belonging to the controlled trustee or to a co-trustee as may be necessary for the purpose of opening or maintaining the account; and

    (c) money to replace any sum which for any reason may have been drawn from the account in contravention of rule 17 of these rules.

14. Where a solicitor holds or receives money which includes money subject to a trust or trusts of which the solicitor is controlled trustee–

    (a) he or she shall where practicable split such money and, if he or she does so, shall deal with each part thereof as if he or she had received a separate sum of money in respect of that part; or

    (b) if he or she does not split the money, he or she may pay it into a client account as permitted by Part I of these rules.

15. No money, other than money which under rules 12 to 14 of these rules a solicitor is required or permitted to pay into a controlled trust account, shall be paid into a controlled trust account, and it shall be the duty of a solicitor into whose controlled trust account any money has been paid in contravention of this rule to withdraw the same without delay on discovery.

16. There may be drawn from a controlled trust account–

    (a) money properly required for a payment in the execution of the particular trust;

    (b) money to be transferred to a client account;

APPENDIX A: SOLICITORS' ACCOUNTS RULES 1991

    (c)   such money, not being money subject to the particular trust, as may have been paid into the account under paragraph (b) of rule 13 of these rules; or

    (d)   money which may for any reason have been paid into the account in contravention of rule 15 of these rules.

17.   No money other than money permitted by rule 16 of these rules to be drawn from a controlled trust account shall be so drawn unless the Council upon an application made to them by the solicitor expressly authorise in writing its withdrawal.

18.   Notwithstanding the provisions of these rules a solicitor shall not be under an obligation to pay into a controlled trust account money held or received by him or her which is subject to a trust of which he or she is controlled trustee–

    (a)   if the money is received by him or her in the form of cash and is without delay paid in cash in the execution of the trust to a third party; or

    (b)   if the money is received by him or her in the form of a cheque or draft which is without delay endorsed over in the execution of the trust to a third party and is not passed by the solicitor through a bank or building society account.

19.   Except in so far as money is dealt with in accordance with Part I of these rules–

    (a)   every controlled trustee shall at all times keep properly written up such accounts as may be necessary–

        (i)   to show separately in respect of each trust of which he or she is controlled trustee all his or her dealings with money received, held or paid by him or her on account of that trust; and

        (ii)   to distinguish the same from money received held or paid by him or her on any other account;

    (b)   every controlled trustee shall preserve for at least six years from the date of the last entry therein all accounts and bank statements;

    (c)   every controlled trustee shall either

        (i)   keep together, centrally, the accounts which he or she is required to keep under this rule 19; or

        (ii)   maintain centrally a register of the trusts in respect of which he or she is required to keep accounts under this rule 19.

COMPLYING WITH THE SOLICITORS' ACCOUNTS RULES: A PRACTICAL GUIDE

Part III – Interest

20. (1) Subject to rule 26 of these rules, a solicitor who holds money for or on account of a client shall account to the client for interest or an equivalent sum in the following circumstances:

   (i) where such money is held on deposit in a separate designated account the solicitor shall account to the client for the interest earned on that money;

   (ii) where such money is not so held on deposit, the solicitor shall, subject to rule 21 of these rules pay to the client out of the solicitor's own money a sum equivalent to the interest which would have accrued if the money received had been so kept on deposit, or its gross equivalent if the interest would have been net of tax.

   (2) In paragraph (1) of this rule, for the avoidance of doubt, the reference to a solicitor who holds money for or on account of a client includes the solicitor holding money in his or her capacity as solicitor on account of the trustees of a trust (other than a controlled trust) of which the solicitor is a trustee.

21. A solicitor shall only be required to account in accordance with rule 20(1)(ii) of these rules where:

   (i) the solicitor holds the money for as long as or longer than the number of weeks set out in the left hand column of the table below and the minimum amount held equals or exceeds the corresponding figure in the right hand column of the table;

   TABLE

No. of weeks	Minimum amount
8	£ 1,000
4	£ 2,000
2	£10,000
1	£20,000

   or

   (ii) the solicitor holds a sum of money exceeding £20,000 for less than one week and it is fair and reasonable to so account having regard to all the circumstances; or

APPENDIX A: SOLICITORS' ACCOUNTS RULES 1991

    (iii) the solicitor holds money continuously which varies significantly in amount over the period during which it is held and it is fair and reasonable so to account having regard to any sum payable under paragraph (i) of this rule and to the varying amounts of money and length of time for which these are held; or

    (iv) the solicitor holds sums of money intermittently during the course of acting and it is fair and reasonable so to account having regard to all the circumstances including the aggregate of the sums held and the periods for which they are held notwithstanding that no individual sum would have attracted interest under paragraph (i) of this rule; or

    (v) rule 22 of these rules applies.

22. Where money is held by a solicitor for or on account of a client for a continuous period and the money is held on deposit in a separate designated account for only part of that period, and no interest would be payable for the rest of the period under rule 21(i) to (iii) of these rules, the solicitor shall:

    (i) for the part of the period during which the money was so held on deposit, account for interest in accordance with rule 20(1)(i) of these rules; and

    (ii) for the rest of the period, pay interest where it is fair and reasonable to do so having regard to all the circumstances including the interest which would have been payable under rule 21(i) to (iii) if the money had been kept off deposit for the whole of the period.

23. For the purposes of rule 20(1)(ii) of these rules the sum payable to the client shall be calculated by reference to the interest payable on a separate designated account:

    (i) at the bank or building society where the money is held; or

    (ii) where the money, or part of it, is held in successive and concurrent accounts maintained at different banks or building societies, at whichever of those banks or building societies was offering the highest rate of interest on such account on the day when the sum payable under rule 20(1)(ii) commenced to accrue; or

    (iii) where, contrary to the provisions of Parts I and II of these rules, the money is not held in a client account, at any bank or building society nominated by the client.

COMPLYING WITH THE SOLICITORS' ACCOUNTS RULES: A PRACTICAL GUIDE

24. Subject to rule 26(c) of these rules, where a solicitor holds money as a stakeholder (whether or not such money is paid by a client of the solicitor) the solicitor shall pay interest in accordance with Part III of these rules save that such interest shall be paid to the person to whom the stake is paid.

25. Without prejudice to any other remedy which may be available to him or her, any client who feels aggrieved that interest or a sum equivalent thereto has not been paid to him or her under Part III of these rules shall be entitled to apply to the Law Society for a certificate as to whether or not interest ought to have been earned for him or her and, if so, the amount of such interest; and upon the issue of such a certificate the sum certified to be due shall be payable by the solicitor to the client.

26. Nothing in Part III of these rules shall:

   (a) affect any arrangement in writing, whenever made, between a solicitor and his or her client as to the application of the client's money or interest thereon;

   (b) apply to money received by a solicitor:

   (i) being money subject to a controlled trust; or

   (ii) in his or her capacity as trustee rather than as solicitor, on account of the trustees of any other trust of which the solicitor is a trustee;

   (c) affect any agreement in writing for payment of interest on stakeholder money held by a solicitor.

Part IV – Compliance

27. (1) In order to ascertain whether Parts I, II and III of these rules have been complied with the Council, acting either–

   (a) on their own motion; or

   (b) on a written statement and request transmitted to them by or on behalf of the Governing Body of a Local Law Society or a Committee thereof; or

   (c) on a written complaint lodged with them by a third party,

   may require any solicitor, either in the solicitor's capacity as solicitor or controlled trustee, to produce at a time and place to be fixed by the Council, the solicitor's books of account, bank and building society statements, pass-books, loose-leaf bank and building society statements of account, vouchers and any other necessary documents, including any documents relating to all or any of the trusts of which a solicitor is controlled trustee, for the inspection of any person appointed by the Council and to supply to such person any necessary information and explanations and such person shall be directed to prepare for the information of the Council a report on the result of such inspection. Such report may be used as a basis for proceedings under the Solicitors Act 1974.

(2) Upon being required so to do a solicitor shall produce such books of account, bank and building society pass books, loose-leaf bank and building society statements, statements of account, vouchers and documents at the time and place fixed.

(3) In any case in which the Governing Body of a Local Law Society or a Committee thereof are of the opinion that an inspection should be made under this rule of the books of account, bank and building society pass books, loose-leaf bank and building society statements, statements of account, vouchers and any other necessary documents of a solicitor, including any documents relating to all or any of the trusts of which a solicitor is controlled trustee, it shall be the duty of such Governing Body or Committee to transmit to the Council a statement containing all relevant information in their possession and a request that such an inspection be made.

(4) Before instituting an inspection on a written complaint lodged with them by a third party, the Council shall require *prima facie* evidence that a ground of complaint exists, and may require the payment by such party to the Council of a reasonable sum to be fixed by them to cover the costs of the inspection and the costs of the solicitor against whom the complaint is made. The Council may deal with any sum so paid in such manner as they think fit.

(5) Where a requirement is made by the Council of a recognised body under this rule 27, such requirement shall, if so stated in the requirement, be deemed also to be made of any solicitor who is an officer or employee of that recognised body where, respectively, such solicitor holds or has held client's money or is or has been a controlled trustee.

28. (1) Every requirement to be made by the Council of a solicitor or controlled trustee as the case may be under these rules shall be made in writing, and left at or sent by registered post or the recorded delivery service to the last address of the solicitor appearing in the Roll or in the Register kept by the Society under section 9 of the Solicitors Act 1974. If the requirement is so made and sent, it shall be deemed to have been received by the solicitor within forty-eight hours (excluding Saturdays, Sundays and Bank Holidays) of the time of posting.

(2) For the purposes of rule 28(1) of these rules, the reference to the last address of a solicitor or a controlled trustee appearing in the Roll or in the Register kept by the Society under section 9 of the Solicitors Act 1974 shall be construed, in relation to:

(i) a recognised body or a recognised body which is a controlled trustee, as a reference to the registered office of the recognised body last communicated to the Council or the Society under the Solicitors' Incorporated Practice Rules 1988 (or any rules for the time being replacing those rules); and

(ii) a registered foreign lawyer, or a registered foreign lawyer who is a controlled trustee, as a reference to the address of the registered foreign lawyer appearing in the register kept under section 89 of the Courts and Legal Services Act 1990.

29. Nothing in these rules shall deprive a solicitor of any recourse or right, whether by way of lien, set off, counterclaim, charge or otherwise, against moneys standing to the credit of a client account or controlled trust account.

Part V – Application

30. These rules shall not apply to a solicitor acting in the course of his or her employment as (a) a public officer, or (b) an officer of statutory undertakers, or (c) an officer of a local authority.

31. (1) These rules shall apply to a recognised body, and to a registered foreign lawyer practising as a member of a multi-national partnership or as the director of a recognised body, as they apply to a solicitor.

APPENDIX A: SOLICITORS' ACCOUNTS RULES 1991

(2) In rules 2-30 of these rules, "solicitor" shall, in addition to the meanings set out in the definition in rule 2(1) of these rules, also include a registered foreign lawyer practising as a member of a multi-national partnership or as the director of a recognised body, and a multi-national partnership.

(3) Notwithstanding paragraph (2) of this rule, the definition of a "controlled trustee" in rule 2(1) of these rules shall not include a registered foreign lawyer.

(4) In these rules:

   (a) "controlled trustee" shall include:

      (i) a registered foreign lawyer who is a member of a multi-national partnership and who is a sole trustee or co-trustee only with one or more of the employees or other partners of that partnership and who is trustee by virtue of being a member of that partnership; and

      (ii) a registered foreign lawyer who is the director of a recognised body and who is a sole trustee or co-trustee only with one or more other officers or employees of that recognised body or the body itself and who is trustee by virtue of practising as a director of that body; and

   (b) "multi-national partnership" and "registered foreign lawyer" shall have the meanings given in section 89 of the Courts and Legal Services Act 1990.

APPENDIX B
Solicitors' Accounts (Legal Aid Temporary Provision) Rule 1992

Rule dated 8 May 1992 made by the Council of the Law Society with the concurrence, where requisite, of the Master of the Rolls pursuant to section 32 of the Solicitors Act 1974 and section 9 of the Administration of Justice Act 1985, regulating the keeping of accounts by solicitors, registered foreign lawyers and recognised bodies in respect of their English and Welsh practices.

Receipt of legal aid payments which include unpaid professional disbursements

(1) This rule is supplemental to the Solicitors' Accounts Rules 1991 and may be cited as the Solicitors' Accounts (Legal Aid Temporary Provision) Rule 1992. It shall come into operation on the 1st day of June 1992.

(2) In this rule:

    (a) "office account" shall mean a bank or building society account in the name of a solicitor which is kept, maintained or operated by the solicitor in connection with his or her practice, not being a client account or controlled trust account;

    (b) all other expressions shall, unless the context otherwise requires, have the meanings assigned to them by rule 2 of the Solicitors' Accounts Rules 1991.

(3) When a solicitor receives from the Legal Aid Board a payment in respect of costs, all or part of which relates to the unpaid fees of another lawyer, professional or other agent, or expert instructed by the solicitor, the solicitor may, notwithstanding rules 3 and 5 of the Solicitors' Accounts Rules 1991, elect to pay the whole of the payment without delay into an office account *provided that* within fourteen days of receipt the solicitor transfers to a client account any part of the payment which relates to such fees still remaining unpaid.

(4) This rule shall, for the purposes of the Accountant's Report Rules 1991, be deemed to form part of Part I of the Solicitors' Accounts Rules 1991.

APPENDIX C
Accountant's Report Rules 1991

(WITH CONSOLIDATED AMENDMENTS TO 1 JUNE 1996)

[Note: Amendments coming into force on 1 September 1998 are shown in italics within square brackets.]

Rules dated 11 July 1991 made by the Council of the Law Society pursuant to section 34 of the Solicitors Act 1974, section 9 of the Administration of Justice Act 1985 and schedule 15 paragraph 6 of the Financial Services Act 1986 with respect to the delivery of accountants' reports by solicitors, registered foreign lawyers and recognised bodies in respect of their English and Welsh practices.

1. These rules may be cited as the Accountant's Report Rules 1991, and shall come into operation on the 1st day of June, 1992, whereupon the Accountant's Report Rules 1986 shall cease to have effect save in relation to reports covering periods prior to 1 June 1992.

2. In these rules:

    (1) the expressions "client's money", "client", "trust money", "controlled trust", "controlled trust account", "recognised body", "separate designated account" and "client account" shall have the meanings respectively assigned to them by the Solicitors' Accounts Rules 1991, but in the case of a solicitor holding one of the offices to which rule 30 of the Solicitors' Accounts Rules 1991, or subsection (2) of section 88 of the Solicitors Act 1974 applies, "client's money" shall not extend to money held or received by the solicitor in the course of his or her employment in such office;

    (2) "solicitor" means a solicitor of the Supreme Court and shall include a recognised body;

    (3) words in the singular include the plural, words in the plural include the singular and words importing the masculine or feminine shall include the neuter;

(4) (i) a reference to the Solicitors' Accounts Rules 1991 includes any modification or amendment or re-enactment thereof;

(ii) a reference to the Solicitors' Investment Business Rules 1990 includes any modification or amendment or re-enactment thereof;

(5) other expressions shall except where otherwise stated have the meanings assigned to them by the Solicitors Act 1974.

3. (1) An accountant shall be qualified to give an accountant's report on behalf of a solicitor if–

(a) he or she is a member of–

(i) The Institute of Chartered Accountants in England and Wales; or

(ii) The Institute of Chartered Accountants of Scotland; or

(iii) The Chartered Association of Certified Accountants; or

(iv) The Institute of Chartered Accountants in Ireland; or

(v) The Association of Authorised Public Accountants; and

[*(aa) he or she is either*

(i) an individual who is a registered auditor within the terms of section 35(1)(a) of the Companies Act 1989; or

(ii) an employee of such an individual; or

(iii) a partner in or employee of a partnership which is a registered auditor within the terms of section 35(1)(a) of the Companies Act 1989; or

(iv) a director or employee of a company which is a registered auditor within the terms of section 35(1)(a) of the Companies Act 1989; and]

(b) he or she has neither been at any time during the accounting period to which the report relates, nor subsequently, before giving the report, become a partner or employee of such solicitor or any partner of the solicitor; and

(c) he or she is not employed by the same non-solicitor employer as such solicitor; and

(d) he or she is not subject to notice of disqualification under paragraph (2) of this rule.

(2) In either of the following cases, that is to say, where–

(a) the accountant has been found guilty by the Disciplinary Tribunal of his or her professional body of professional misconduct or discreditable conduct; or

(b) the Council are satisfied that a solicitor has not complied with the provisions of Part I or Part II of the Solicitors' Accounts Rules 1991, in respect of matters not specified in an accountant's report and that the accountant was negligent in giving such report, whether or not an application be made for a grant out of the Compensation Fund;

the Council may at their discretion, at any time notify the accountant concerned that he or she is not qualified to give an accountant's report, and they may give notice of such fact to any solicitor on whose behalf he or she may have given an accountant's report, or who may appear to the Council to be likely to employ such accountant for the purpose of giving an accountant's report and cause notice of such fact to be publicised in the Law Society's *Gazette* or similar publication. After such accountant shall have been so notified, unless and until such notice of disqualification shall have been withdrawn by the Council, he or she shall not be qualified to give an accountant's report. Before coming to their decision the Council shall take into consideration any observations or explanation made or given by such accountant or on his or her behalf by the professional body of which he or she is a member.

(3) Rule 3(1)(b) of this rule shall have effect in relation to the qualification of an accountant to give an accountant's report on behalf of a recognised body as if for "of such solicitor or any partner of the solicitor" were substituted "or officer (i) of such recognised body or any partner of its or (ii) of any person who or which is an officer, member or employee of such recognised body or of which such recognised body is an officer or member".

[(4) *The solicitor shall ensure that the reporting accountant's rights and duties are stated in a letter of engagement, which shall incorporate the terms set out in the Second Schedule to these rules. The letter of engagement and a copy shall be signed by the solicitor (or by a partner or director) and by the accountant. The solicitor shall keep the copy of the signed letter of engagement for three years and produce it to the Society on request.*

(5) *Upon instructing an accountancy practice to replace that previously instructed to produce accountant's reports, the solicitor shall immediately notify the Society of the change and provide the name and business address of the new accountancy practice.]*

4. (1) For the purpose of giving an accountant's report, an accountant shall ascertain from the solicitor particulars of all bank and building society accounts (including controlled trust accounts and other accounts which are not client accounts) kept, maintained or operated by the solicitor in connection with his or her practice at any time during the accounting period to which the report relates and subject to paragraph (2) of this rule make the following examination of the books, accounts and other relevant documents of the solicitor:

(A) relating to accounts other than controlled trust accounts–

    (a) so examine the book-keeping system in every office of the solicitor as to enable the accountant to verify that such system complies with rule 11 of the Solicitors' Accounts Rules 1991, and in respect of those solicitors authorised in the conduct of investment business by the Law Society, rules 14 and 26 of the Solicitors' Investment Business Rules 1995, and is so designed that–

        (i) an appropriate ledger account is kept for each client;

        (ii) such ledger accounts show separately from other information particulars of all clients' money received, held or paid on account of each client;

        (iii) transactions relating to clients' money and any other money dealt with through a client account are recorded in the solicitor's books so as to distinguish such transactions from transactions relating to any other money received, held or paid by the solicitor;

(b) make test checks of postings to clients' ledger accounts from records of receipts and payments of clients' money and make test checks of the casts of such accounts and records;

(c) compare a sample of lodgments into and payments from the client account as shown in bank and building society statements with the solicitor's records of receipts and payments of clients' money;

(d) enquire into and test check the system of recording costs and of making transfers in respect of costs from the client account;

(e) make a test examination of such documents as he or she shall request the solicitor to produce to him or her with the object of ascertaining and confirming–

  (i) that the financial transactions, (including those giving rise to transfers from one ledger account to another) evidenced by such documents, are in accordance with Part I of the Solicitors' Accounts Rules 1991 and

  (ii) that the entries in the books of account reflect those transactions in a manner complying with Part I of the Solicitors' Accounts Rules 1991;

(f) subject to paragraph (3) of this rule extract (or check extractions of) balances on the clients' ledger accounts during the accounting period under review at not fewer than two dates selected by the accountant (one of which may be the last day of the accounting period), and at each such date–

  (i) compare the total as shown by such ledger accounts of the liabilities to the clients, including those for whom trust money is held in the client account, with the cash account balance; and

  (ii) reconcile that cash account balance with the balances held in client account and elsewhere as confirmed direct to the accountant by the relevant banks and building societies or other institutions;

(g) satisfy himself or herself that reconciliation statements have been kept in accordance with rule 11(5) of the Solicitors' Accounts Rules 1991;

COMPLYING WITH THE SOLICITORS' ACCOUNTS RULES: A PRACTICAL GUIDE

(h) make a test examination of the clients' ledger accounts in order to ascertain whether payments from the client account have been made on any individual account in excess of money held on behalf of that client;

(i) check such office ledger and cash accounts and bank and building society statements as the solicitor maintains with a view to ascertaining whether any client's money has not been paid into a client account;

(j) check the books of account which contain details of client's money which, with the client's consent, is not held in a client account, to ascertain what transactions have been effected in respect of such account;

(k) make a test examination of the clients' ledger accounts in order to ascertain whether rule 11(3) of the Solicitors' Accounts Rules 1991 has been complied with;

(l) ask for such information and explanations as he or she may require arising out of sub-paragraphs (a) to (k) of this paragraph;

(B) relating to controlled trust accounts–

(a) ascertain from the solicitor details of the record-keeping system(s);

(b) select a limited number of controlled trust matters and in relation to those:

(i) make test checks of postings to the accounts kept pursuant to rule 19 of the Solicitors' Accounts Rules 1991 from records of receipts and payments of money and test checks of the casts of such accounts and records;

(ii) make a test examination of such documents as he or she shall request the solicitor to produce with the object of ascertaining and confirming that both the financial transactions evidenced by those documents and the entries in the accounting records reflecting those transactions are in accordance with Part II of the Solicitors' Accounts Rules 1991;

(iii) enquire into and test check the system of recording costs and of making transfers in respect of costs;

APPENDIX C: ACCOUNTANT'S REPORT RULES 1991

    (iv)   compare the balance at the last day of the accounting period under review as shown by the records kept under rule 19 of the Solicitors' Accounts Rules 1991 with the balance on each controlled trust account as confirmed direct to the accountant by the bank(s) and building society(ies);

    (v)   request such information and explanations as the accountant may require arising out of sub-paragraphs (i)-(iv).

(2) Nothing in paragraph (1) of this rule shall require the accountant–

    (a)   to extend his or her enquiries beyond the information contained in the relevant documents relating to any client's matter produced to him or her supplemented by such information and explanations as he or she may obtain from the solicitor;

    (b)   to enquire into the stocks, shares, other securities or documents of title held by the solicitor on behalf of the solicitor's clients;

    (c)   to consider whether the books of account of the solicitor have been properly written up in accordance with rules 11 and 19 of the Solicitors' Accounts Rules 1991, at any time other than the time as at which his or her examination of those books and accounts takes place.

(3) In so far as rule 4(1)(A)(f) of these rules requires an accountant to extract, or check extractions of, balances on the clients' ledger accounts then, where a solicitor uses a computerised or mechanised system of accounting which automatically produces an extraction of all client ledger balances, in so far as such work merely amounts to a check on the accuracy of the computer or machine, the accountant shall not be required to check all client ledger balances extracted on the list produced by the computer or machine against the individual records of ledger accounts, provided the accountant:

    (a)   is satisfied that a satisfactory system of control is in operation and the books are in balance;

    (b)   carries out a test check of the extraction against the individual records; and

    (c)   specifies in his or her report that he or she has relied on the exception set out in this rule 4(3).

(4) If after making an examination in accordance with paragraphs (1), (2) and (3) of this rule it appears to the accountant that there is evidence that Part I or Part II of the Solicitors' Accounts Rules 1991 has not been complied with the accountant shall make such further examination as he or she considers necessary in order to complete the report with or without qualification.

(5) Except where a client's money has been deposited in a separate designated account, nothing in these rules shall apply to any matter arising under section 33 of the Solicitors Act 1974 or Part III of the Solicitors' Accounts Rules 1991, notwithstanding any payment into client account of a sum in lieu of interest.

5. Nothing in these rules shall deprive a solicitor of the right on the grounds of privilege as between solicitor and client to decline to produce to the accountant any document which the accountant may consider it necessary for him to inspect for the purposes of his or her examination in accordance with rule 4 of these rules and where the solicitor so declines, the accountant shall qualify the report to that effect setting out the circumstances.

6. An accountant's report delivered by a solicitor under these rules shall be in the form set out in the [*First*] Schedule to these rules or in a form to the like effect approved by the Council.

[6A. *The accountant should exercise his or her professional judgement in adopting a suitable 'audit' programme, but shall also complete and sign the checklist produced from time to time by the Society. The solicitor shall retain the completed checklist for three years and produce it to the Society on request.*

6B. *The accountant should be aware of the Society's current Guidelines for Procedures and Systems for Accounting, and shall note in the accountant's report any substantial departures from the Guidelines discovered during the course of carrying out work in preparation of the report.*]

7. (1) A solicitor need not deliver an accountant's report during a practice year if:

(a) the solicitor did not hold or receive client's money or money subject to a controlled trust at any time during the previous practice year; or

(b) having held or received client's money or money subject to a controlled trust during the previous practice year, the solicitor has ceased so to do and has delivered an accountant's report which confirms this; or

APPENDIX C: ACCOUNTANT'S REPORT RULES 1991

    (c)   the solicitor is exempt from complying with the Solicitors' Accounts Rules 1991 by virtue of rule 30 of those rules or section 88 (2) of the Solicitors Act 1974.

(2)   If a solicitor has been held out as a partner of another solicitor who has held or received client's money or money subject to a controlled trust that solicitor shall be deemed also to have held or received such money.

(3)   (a)   Rule 7(1) shall not have effect in respect of the delivery of an accountant's report by a recognised body.

    (b)   The Council will in each practice year be satisfied that the delivery of an accountant's report is unnecessary in the case of any recognised body which:

        (i)   did not hold or receive client's money or money subject to a controlled trust during the preceding practice year and which within three months of the end of such year delivers to the Council a declaration to that effect signed by a director of the body; or

        (ii)   having held or received client's money or money subject to a controlled trust during the preceding practice year, has ceased so to do and has delivered an accountant's report which confirms this; or

        (iii)   is exempt from complying with the Solicitors' Accounts Rules 1991 by virtue of rule 30 of those rules or section 88(2) of the Solicitors Act 1974.

8.   (1)   In the case of a solicitor who—

    (a)   becomes under an obligation to deliver his or her first accountant's report; or

    (b)   having been exempt under rule 7 of these rules from delivering an accountant's report in the preceding practice year, becomes under an obligation to deliver an accountant's report;

the accounting period shall begin on the date upon which he or she first held or received client's money or money subject to a controlled trust or, after such exemption, began again to hold or receive client's money or money subject to a controlled trust, and may cover less than twelve months, and shall in all other respects comply with the requirements of subsection (3) of section 34 of the Solicitors Act 1974.

(2) In the case of a solicitor retiring from practice who, having ceased to hold or receive client's money or money subject to a controlled trust, is under an obligation to deliver his or her final accountant's report, the accounting period shall end on the date upon which the solicitor ceased to hold or receive client's money or money subject to a controlled trust, and may cover less than twelve months, and shall in all other respects comply with the requirements of subsection (3) of section 34 of the Solicitors Act 1974.

(3) The reference in rule 8(2) to a solicitor retiring from practice shall be construed as including a reference to a recognised body ceasing to practise [, *and to a solicitor ceasing to hold or receive client's money or money subject to a controlled trust but otherwise continuing in practice*].

9. (1) In the case of a solicitor who–

(a) was not exempt under rule 7 of these rules from delivering an accountant's report in the preceding practice year; and

(b) since the expiry of the accounting period covered by such accountant's report has become, or ceased to be, a member of a firm of solicitors,

the accounting period may cover less than twelve months and shall in all other respects comply with the requirements of subsection (3) of section 34 of the Solicitors Act 1974.

(2) In the case of a solicitor who has two or more places of business–

(a) separate accounting periods covered by separate accountant's reports may be adopted in respect of each such place of business, provided that the accounting periods comply with the requirements of subsection (3) of section 34 of the Solicitors Act 1974; and

(b) the accountant's report or the accountant's reports delivered by the solicitor to the Society in each practice year shall cover all client's money or money subject to a controlled trust held or received by him or her.

10. (1) Every notice to be given by the Council under these rules to a solicitor shall be in writing and left at or sent by registered post or the recorded delivery service to the last address of the solicitor appearing on the Roll or in the Register kept by the Society under section 9 of the

APPENDIX C: ACCOUNTANT'S REPORT RULES 1991

Solicitors Act 1974. If the notice is so given and sent, it shall be deemed to have been received by the solicitor within forty-eight hours (excluding Saturdays, Sundays and Bank Holidays) of the time of posting.

(2) For the purpose of rule 10(1) of these rules, the reference to the last address of a solicitor appearing on the Roll or in the Register kept by the Society under section 9 of the Solicitors Act 1974 shall be construed, in relation to:

(i) a recognised body, as a reference to the registered office of the recognised body last communicated to the Council or the Society under the Solicitors' Incorporated Practice Rules 1988 (or any rules for the time being replacing those rules); and

(ii) a registered foreign lawyer, as a reference to the address of the registered foreign lawyer appearing in the register kept under section 89 of the Courts and Legal Services Act 1990.

11. Every notice to be given by the Council under these rules to an accountant shall be in writing and left at or sent by registered post or the recorded delivery service to the address of the accountant as shown on an accountant's report or appearing in the records of the professional body of which the accountant is a member, and, when so given and delivered or sent, shall be deemed to have been received by the accountant within forty-eight hours (excluding Saturdays, Sundays and Bank Holidays) of the time of delivery or posting.

11A. (1) These rules shall apply to a recognised body, and to a registered foreign lawyer practising as a member of a multi-national partnership or as the director of a recognised body, as they apply to a solicitor.

(2) There shall be no requirement for a registered foreign lawyer to deliver an accountant's report in respect of any period in which he or she was not practising as set out in paragraph (1) of this rule.

(3) In rules 2-10 of these rules, "solicitor" shall, in addition to the meanings given in rule 2(2) of these rules, also include a registered foreign lawyer practising as set out in paragraph (1) of this rule.

(4) In these rules, "multi-national partnership" and "registered foreign lawyer" shall have the meanings given in section 89 of the Courts and Legal Services Act 1990.

12. The Council shall have power to waive in writing in any particular case any of the provisions of these rules.

THE [FIRST] SCHEDULE
ACCOUNTANT'S REPORT

[The form of report is prepared and issued by the Society and is not reproduced here.]

[THE SECOND SCHEDULE
TERMS TO BE INCORPORATED IN LETTER OF ENGAGEMENT

In accordance with rule 3(4) of the Accountant's Report Rules 1991, you are instructed as follows:

(i) *that you may, and are encouraged to, report directly to the Law Society without prior reference to me/this firm/this company should you, during the course of carrying out work in preparation of the accountant's report, discover evidence of theft or fraud affecting client's money or money subject to a controlled trust, or information which is likely to be of material significance in determining whether any solicitor, registered foreign lawyer or recognised body is a fit and proper person to hold client's money or money subject to a controlled trust;*

(ii) *to report directly to the Law Society should your appointment be terminated following the issue of, or indication of intention to issue, a qualified accountant's report, or following the raising of concerns prior to the preparation of an accountant's report;*

(iii) *to deliver to me/this firm/this company with your report the completed checklist required by rule 6A of the Accountant's Report Rules 1991; to retain for three years a copy of the completed checklist; and to produce the copy to the Law Society on request;*

(iv) *to retain these terms of engagement for three years and to produce them to the Law Society on request; and*

(v) *following any direct report made to the Law Society under (i) or (ii) above, to provide to the Law Society on request any further relevant information in your possession or in the possession of your firm.*

To the extent necessary to enable you to comply with (i)-(v) above, I/we waive my/the firm's/the company's right of confidentiality. This waiver extends to any report made, document produced or information disclosed to the Law Society in good faith pursuant to these instructions, even though it may subsequently transpire that you were mistaken in your belief that there was cause for concern.]

APPENDIX D

Guidance on the requirements under Rule 8(2) of the Solicitors' Accounts Rules 1991

The Council's current policy requires that applicants must provide:

1. Details of the amounts in question together with an indication of the interest accrued.
2. Details of attempts made to trace the proper destination of the money. It must be shown (a) that adequate attempts have been made or (b) the reasonable costs of doing so are likely to be excessively high in relation to the money held.
3. Evidence that a period of six years has elapsed since the money was due to the client.
4. A letter from the firm's accountants confirming that they are satisfied that the money referred to is held on behalf of a particular client who the firm has been unable to trace.
5. An indication of the destination of the money, should the Council grant authority.
6. If you are dealing with the administration of an estate, the executors and administrators have the authority to deal with the unclaimed sums or monies which remain outstanding.

It should be noted that a firm would remain liable to account to the rightful claimant, if he or she should reappear. If the money is donated to the Solicitors Benevolent Association, the Association will be able to give an indemnity in the event that a claim is made against the donor. Solicitors wishing to make an application under Rule 8 should write to the Professional Ethics Division, Professional Standards Directorate, Ipsley Court, Berrington Close, Redditch B98 0TD

The Standards and Guidance Casework Committee cannot grant a waiver under Rule 8(2) in respect of any trust monies.

APPENDIX E
Guidance on deposit interest – Solicitors' Accounts Rules 1991, Part III

Introduction

1. The rules on deposit interest ('the deposit interest provisions') appear in Part III of the Solicitors' Accounts Rules 1991 (see Annex 28B in *The Guide to the Professional Conduct of Solicitors 1996* (the Guide)). The Society receives a number of enquiries from solicitors on two points in particular:

    A. What is the rate of interest which should be paid under the deposit interest provisions? and

    B. Is it permissible to enter into written agreements with clients to disapply the deposit interest provisions?

2. It should be noted that the deposit interest provisions do not apply to money subject to a controlled trust (i.e. a trust where the solicitor is sole trustee or co-trustee only with one or more partners or employees). This guidance applies only to categories of money covered by the deposit interest provisions, i.e. money held or received on account of the firm's clients: including (i) stakeholder money; and (ii) money held or received on account of a trust where the solicitor is trustee with others outside the firm (assuming, as will normally be the case, that the solicitor holds or receives the money in his or her capacity as solicitor).

3. Where the deposit interest provisions do not apply (as in the case of money subject to a controlled trust), all interest should normally be credited to the relevant trust in accordance with the general law.

A. Rates of interest

4. Rule 20(1) of the Solicitors' Accounts Rules 1991 provides that a solicitor who holds money for or on account of a client must account to that client for either:

APPENDIX E: GUIDANCE – DEPOSIT INTEREST

    (i)   all interest earned (in the case of a separate designated account) or

    (ii)   an equivalent sum (in the case of a general client account), based on the interest which would have been earned if the money held for that client had been kept on deposit in a separate designated account. Rule 20(1) follows section 33(1) of the Solicitors Act 1974.

5.   All interest earned on a separate designated account must be paid to the client, but the obligation to pay an equivalent sum for amounts held on general client account is subject to the *de minimis* provisions contained in rule 21. It should also be noted that section 33(3) of the Solicitors Act 1974 permits solicitors to retain any interest earned on general client account over and above that which they are obliged to pay to their clients under the deposit interest provisions.

6.   Neither section 33 of the Solicitors Act 1974 nor rule 20(1) specifies particular rates of interest. Instead, reference is made to interest actually earned on deposit in a separate designated account, or to 'a sum equivalent to the interest which would have accrued' had the money been kept on deposit in a separate designated account.

7.   In relation to the second category, the sum payable to the client is normally calculated by reference to the interest payable on a separate designated account at the bank or building society where the money is held (rule 23(i)), i.e. the bank or building society where the solicitor keeps his or her general client account.

8.   Banks and building societies offer many different accounts with varying bands of interest. The rates of interest available for businesses may be lower than the deposit rates available to the general public, particularly for smaller deposits. Some, but not all, of the apparent difference may result from interest being credited quarterly on business accounts and only annually on accounts available to the general public.

9.   It should also be remembered that interest may be set at even lower rates for individual businesses to offset other benefits. For example, a solicitor might prefer not to be charged for telegraphic transfers or drawing cheques, and this might be reflected in the rates of interest paid on the solicitor's client accounts. It is not therefore considered appropriate simply to look at the rate actually being paid to the solicitor, given that this could be kept artificially low. Rather, it would be appropriate to consider the rate or range of rates available to the bank's solicitor customers generally. *Prima facie*, separate designated accounts are business accounts. However, if the bank treats such accounts as personal accounts and pays interest accordingly, that would be the appropriate rate of interest in calculating a 'sum equivalent'.

10. It is normal for banks and building societies to offer accounts which provide instant access to savings in conjunction with competitive rates of interest. It may, however, be relevant to consider whether the sum held on general client account would have been paid into an instant access or longer-term deposit account, had the solicitor placed it in a separate designated account. When instant access is important, this can be taken into account in assessing the appropriate rate of interest to be paid, if the solicitor's bank pays at different rates on instant access accounts. The converse applies where the money is unlikely to be required at short notice. However, a solicitor is not expected to have the benefit of hindsight.

11. Solicitors should be aware that many banks operate deposit accounts with rates of interest as low as 1.75%, regardless of the amount deposited, and may place any sum of money earmarked for deposit in such an account, unless the solicitor stipulates otherwise. This practice is followed despite the existence of other deposit accounts which pay higher 'stepped' rates to reflect the sums invested, and is obviously for the benefit of the bank concerned.

12. It would seem inconceivable that a court would consider that a solicitor had fulfilled his or her obligations to a client by placing a reasonably large sum for any length of time in a separate designated account yielding a very low rate of interest. Similarly, it is inappropriate for a solicitor to calculate the 'sum equivalent' for monies kept in a general client account by looking at accounts yielding such low rates of interest. On the other hand, solicitors would not normally be obliged to pay at a higher rate than they themselves receive on general client account, unless that rate is being kept artificially low, or unless the bank routinely pays a higher rate on separate designated accounts. Furthermore, solicitors are not required to pay the interest which the client himself or herself could have obtained.

13. In summary, solicitors should aim to obtain a reasonable rate of interest for clients on any separate designated account, and to account to their clients for a fair rate of interest on monies kept in general client account. The rate of interest may not be the highest rate obtainable but it is not acceptable simply to look at the lowest rate of interest obtainable.

B. *Contracting out of the deposit interest provisions*

Partial contracting out

14. Rule 20 is subject to rule 26(a) which, in accordance with section 33(4) of the Solicitors Act 1974, states that:

APPENDIX E: GUIDANCE – DEPOSIT INTEREST

'Nothing in Part III of these rules shall

(a) affect any arrangement in writing, whenever made, between a solicitor and his or her client as to the application of the client's money or interest thereon'.

On the face of it, therefore, it seems that a solicitor is entitled to contract out of the deposit interest provisions. However, this guidance demonstrates that caution should be exercised in this respect.

15. Rule 21(i) contains the *de minimis* provisions relating to deposit interest. These provisions operate by way of a table setting out minimum amounts and lengths of time for which money has to be held before interest becomes payable. They should not be confused with rule 10 of the Solicitors' Practice Rules 1990 (see 14.14 in the Guide), which deals with *commission* received from third parties and provides that solicitors must normally account to the client for any commission received of more than £20.

16. When the Council looked at the deposit interest provisions in 1992, interest rates for savings between £500 and £25,000 appeared to average 6%–8%. An example was given of the way in which the table contained in rule 21(i) of the Accounts Rules would work, using a 6% interest rate for sums below £10,000 and a 7$^{1}/2$% interest rate for sums of and above £10,000. These figures are set out below:

Interest rate	Number of weeks	Minimum amount	Interest payable
6% x	8/52 x	£1,000 =	£9.23
6% x	4/52 x	£2,000 =	£9.23
7$^{1}/2$% x	2/52 x	£10,000 =	£28.85
7$^{1}/2$% x	1/52 x	£20,000 =	£28.85

The average of these figures is £19.04. The aim of rule 21 is that the deposit interest provisions should provide an average *de minimis* sum of approximately £20.

17. However, interest rates change regularly and where rates fall the sums payable at the lower end of the table may not always be high enough to justify the expense of accounting to clients. As an alternative to using the table solicitors may prefer to stipulate in standard terms of business a £20 *de minimis* exception for all sums held by them. This is acceptable.

18. Some solicitors have computerised systems which produce calculations of deposit interest due to clients. Many will however produce, say, only four bands of interest rates (whereas banks might offer 10 or more). It is

acceptable to utilise a limited number of bands of interest and to stipulate in standard terms of business that those rates will be applied in the calculation of interest due to the firm's clients, provided that the firm's rates do not result overall in a materially worse position for its clients.

Contracting out altogether

19. Despite the proviso in rule 26(a), it is considered improper for a solicitor to request a client to enter into an arrangement in writing with a view to paying no interest at all. This is because the client is then deprived of his or her entitlement under the deposit interest provisions when he or she is probably in no position to assess the merits of the request and to give informed consent.

20. It has been argued that the deposit interest provisions are similar to the commissions rule which allows a solicitor to keep commission with the client's agreement. There is however a fundamental distinction between rule 10 of the Solicitors' Practice Rules 1990 (commissions rule) and the deposit interest provisions, in that the former only allows a solicitor to keep commission on the basis of full disclosure of the amount or method of calculation. The difficulty in seeking a client's agreement at the outset of the transaction to waive his or her rights under the deposit interest provisions is that it will probably not be known exactly how much money the solicitor will hold or for how long, and the client will thus not be in a position to give informed consent because he or she will not know precisely what rights he or she is being asked to give up. A solicitor might well be found to be in breach of his or her fiduciary duty by seeking such an agreement without affording the client an opportunity to give informed consent.

21. However, there are some cases where it might be appropriate for such an arrangement to be made where there is a *quid pro quo* for the client; for example, where a solicitor acts for a company in numerous debt collection matters, possibly with a float from the company with which to finance cases, and the rate of charge agreed with the client takes into account the fact that no interest is to be paid. There may be other acceptable cases where a special price is fixed for an individual client on the basis that the solicitor will retain interest. In seeking a client's consent to such an arrangement, solicitors will have to be aware of the differing needs of clients; for instance, a client unaccustomed to dealing with solicitors will require more by way of explanation than a commercial client who regularly instructs the firm.

22. In summary, each case should be treated on its merits. Solicitors should act fairly towards their clients and provide sufficient information to enable them to give informed consent where it is felt appropriate to depart from the

APPENDIX E: GUIDANCE – DEPOSIT INTEREST

deposit interest provisions. It would be considered appropriate to contract out of the deposit interest provisions where this is at the request of or for the convenience of the client, or where the client receives some compensating benefit. Contracting out would never be appropriate where it is against the client's interests.

Contracting out – stakeholder money

23. Stakeholder money is subject to rule 24 of the Accounts Rules, and the solicitor must pay interest in accordance with the rules to the person to whom the stake is paid. The Law Society's Standard Conditions of Sale provide at 2.2.3 that a deposit held as stakeholder is held 'on terms that on completion it is paid to the seller with accrued interest'.

24. Rule 24 is subject to rule 26(c) which provides:

    'Nothing in Part III of these rules shall...

    (c) affect any agreement in writing for payment of interest on stakeholder money held by a solicitor'.

    This on the face of it seems to permit the solicitor to obtain an agreement for the solicitor to retain interest instead of paying it to the recipient of the stake. It is not however normal practice for a stakeholder in conveyancing transactions to receive remuneration in this way and solicitors must exercise caution as the following demonstrates.

25. A solicitor stakeholder is entitled to stipulate for a reasonable charge for his or her services. It may in appropriate circumstances be acceptable for solicitors to include a special provision in the contract that the solicitor stakeholder retains the interest on the deposit to cover his or her charges for acting as stakeholder. However, this is only acceptable if it will provide fair and reasonable remuneration for the work and risk involved in holding a stake. The contract could, perhaps, stipulate a maximum charge, with any interest earned above that figure being paid to the recipient of the stake.

26. For an agreement validly to exclude the operation of the rule, three parties must assent to it – the stakeholder, the stakeholder's own client and the other party to the transaction. Proper instructions must be sought from the client. A solicitor should be particularly careful not to take unfair advantage either of his or her client or of the other party where the latter is unrepresented.

November 1992, revised January 1996

APPENDIX F
Guidance on commissions

1. Why did the Society make a rule to prevent solicitors keeping commission unless their clients consent?

Practice rule 10 (see 14.14 in *The Guide to the Professional Conduct of Solicitors 1996* (the Guide)) simply put into practice rule form what had long been required of solicitors both as a matter of law and of professional conduct. The position at law results from the fiduciary and agency relationships which exist between the solicitor and the client. One of the consequences of these relationships is that a solicitor cannot unless otherwise authorised by law, contract or a trust deed, keep a secret remuneration or financial benefit arising from the use of client's property.

2. To what sort of commissions does the rule apply?

Any financial benefit which you obtain by reason of and in the course of the relationship of solicitor and client is caught by the rule. Examples include commission on life policies, stocks and shares, pensions and general insurances such as household contents and fire policies (including renewals). Also caught is a payment made to you for introducing a client to a third party (unless the introduction was unconnected with any particular matter which you were currently or had been handling for the client) or for opening a building society account.

3. What exactly is meant by 'account to' the client?

'Account to' does not mean simply telling the client that you will receive commission. It means that unless the client agrees to you keeping the commission it belongs to and must be paid to the client. In this respect, the general law relating to solicitors requires a higher duty from solicitors than from, for example, others in the financial service industry.

APPENDIX F: GUIDANCE ON COMMISSIONS

4. Why must disclosure be in writing?

To protect the interests of both the solicitor and the client. The rule does not require the client's *consent* to be in writing, but this would be advisable (see next question).

5. Can I write to clients setting out details of the commission I will receive and saying that if I do not hear from them within seven days I will assume that they agree to me keeping the commission?

Firstly it is unlikely that this would constitute the agreement of the client for the purpose of practice rule 10. Secondly, it would be unwise to rely on this as it would be an attempt to impose an agreement on the client unilaterally. The case of *Jordy* v. *Vanderpump* (1920) S.J. 324 made clear that the onus is on the solicitor to show the client's consent. Therefore it is advisable to obtain the client's written consent to keep commission.

6. Exactly what has to be disclosed to the client?

The rule requires that the client be told the amount or basis of calculation of the commission or (if the precise amount or basis cannot be ascertained) an approximation thereof. Although the rule gives you a choice of disclosing the actual amount or the basis of calculation, if the actual amount is known then it should be disclosed to the client when you are seeking consent, bearing in mind your duty to act in the best interests of the client. This is particularly so where the basis of calculation of the commission is very complicated. If the exact amount is not known then the calculation should be explained to the client, and in some cases it may be that an approximation would be more helpful than the basis of the calculation, or should be given as well as the basis of calculation. This may depend on the level of understanding of the client. It is also acceptable for a range to be given into which the amount of the commission is likely to fall, provided that the range is not unreasonably wide.

7. What if the estimate I give turns out to have been too low?

If the commission actually received by you is *materially* in excess of the estimate given by you, or indeed the amount or basis originally disclosed to the client, the rule provides that you must account to the client for the excess. Whether the commission is 'materially in excess' of the original figure will depend on the circumstances of each case, and consideration should be given to the amount of

95

any excess, both on its own and as a proportion of the amount which the client has agreed to you keeping, and the client's financial circumstances. The main reason for the use of the word 'material' in the rule is to avoid situations where the cost to the solicitor of accounting to the client for the excess would be greater than the actual amount of the excess. You may prefer simply to have a policy of accounting for all excesses rather than having to worry about whether the sums involved are materially in excess of the original figure, or it may be possible to use the £20 *de minimis* figure as a guideline (see next question).

8. What is the significance of the £20 figure in the rule?

The £20 figure set out in the rule attempts to define for practical purposes what would be acceptable in law as being *de minimis*.

9. What if I receive a number of commissions of less than £20 in the course of acting for one client?

Whether such commissions can be treated separately for the purposes of the rule will depend on the facts of the particular case. Where the commissions are received in respect of separate transactions they can generally be treated separately. It would be wrong, however, to attempt to split up a transaction for the purpose of creating several commissions of £20 or less as this would not be acting in the best interests of the client. Also the commission would probably not, as a matter of law, be retainable on the basis of the *de minimis* principle. Similarly, you may carry out for a client a number of small transactions as part of a single retainer, each of which results in you receiving a commission of less than £20. It may be difficult to argue that the total of the commission is retainable by you on the *de minimis* principle. Such difficulties could be avoided by obtaining the client's consent to retain the commission at the outset of the retainer.

10. When should the client's consent be obtained?

Although the rule does not contain any specific requirements on timing, as a matter of law the best time to obtain the client's consent is before you do the work which results in the commission being payable. Under the law of contract it is likely to be your agreement to do the work which amounts to the consideration for the client's agreement. Therefore, if the client has not consented when you receive the commission, arguably it belongs to the client. Further, it cannot be in keeping with a duty to act in the best interests of the client for a solicitor, having received a commission, to then seek the client's consent to keep it, when the client is entitled in law to receive it.

APPENDIX F: GUIDANCE ON COMMISSIONS

11. When commissions are received should they be placed on office or client account?

If the client has consented to you retaining the commission then the money belongs to you and can be placed on office account. When no such agreement has been obtained the money is the property of the client and must be placed on client account. However, if you have any outstanding costs against the client in respect of this or any other matter, you may, provided a bill or some other written intimation of costs has been submitted to the client, withdraw from client account the sum of money owed in accordance with rule 7 of the Solicitors' Accounts Rules 1991.

12. If the client does not consent to me keeping the commission can I still charge him or her for the work which leads to the commission being payable?

Yes. If a bill is submitted for an amount equal to the amount of commission received and this cannot be justified by the factors set out in the Solicitors' (Non-Contentious Business) Remuneration Order 1994 (see Annex 14C in the Guide), the bill may be reduced under the remuneration certifying procedure or on taxation. The Order would not apply if there was a non-contentious business agreement under section 57 of the Solicitors Act 1974 (see Annex 14A in the Guide) – although the agreement could be set aside if the court considered it to be unfair or unreasonable.

13. If I am charging the client on a fee basis can I take my fee out of the commission?

Yes, providing that you have not agreed with the client to utilise any commission received for some other specific purpose and providing the client has been sent a bill or some other written intimation of costs. In this situation there is no requirement for prior disclosure of the amount of commission or for the client's agreement, as you are, in effect, accounting to the client for the commission and the offsetting is merely a convenient accounting arrangement.

14. Can I advertise 'free conveyancing' where I propose to offset commission against my fees?

No. See paragraph 5 of the Solicitors' Publicity Code 1990 (Annex 11A in the Guide).

15. What is the position regarding VAT if I offset commission against costs?

Where you receive commission from a third party (e.g. an insurance broker) in connection with making a supply to a client, and the commission is to be set against the fee to be charged to the client, VAT is calculated on the *net* amount of the fee, following the setting off of the commission against the fee.

16. If the client signs a section 57 agreement will this also meet the requirements of rule 10?

Provided the agreement contains disclosure of the amount or basis of calculation of commission and a clause that the client consents to you retaining the commission, there will normally have been compliance with rule 10.

17. Could I choose to offer financial services on a commission only basis?

Yes. At the outset of a transaction you may state that you are only prepared to act on the basis that you retain any or part of any commission received, provided this does not conflict with your duty to act in the best interests of the client. Simply obtaining the client's agreement to you acting on a commission only basis will not satisfy the requirements of rule 10 where the amount or basis of calculation of the commission is not known or an approximation cannot be given. The client's informed consent is still required. A drawback of working on a commission only basis is that you could find that either the most suitable product does not generate a commission, or that the client does not proceed. In such a situation you could only charge a fee for the work done if you had made clear at the outset your intention to do so.

18. What if the client defaults on a life policy and I become liable to repay some of the commission?

This can cause difficulties where you have accounted to the client for the commission. One option is to agree with the client that the client will be liable for the amount which you have to repay. The prospects of recovering from the client may not be very good. Other options would be to come to an agreement with the client for the late payment of the commission to the client (in which case the money should be kept on client account) or for you to elect to receive the commission from the insurer on a non-indemnity basis, in which case the commission is paid to you in instalments and if the client defaults no refund is necessary.

APPENDIX F: GUIDANCE ON COMMISSIONS

19. What if the insurance company prohibits me from passing the commission on to the client?

Some insurance companies have been known to state in their agreements with solicitors that the solicitors must not pass any commission on to their clients. In this case, if you cannot obtain the client's agreement to retain the commission you will normally have to decline to accept the commission, and to charge the client a fee instead. It may be possible for you to offset the commission against your fee, but this will depend on the exact nature of the agreement with the insurance company.

20. Surely if I am acting in the renewal of an insurance policy I am not acting as the client's solicitor but as the agent of the insurance company and therefore I am entitled to the commission?

Wrong. See *Copp* v. *Lynch and Law Life Assurance Co.* (1882) 26 S.J. 348 where it was held that the plaintiff was acting as the defendant's solicitor upon renewal of a life policy, and not as agent for the insurance company. Where solicitors are instructed by insurance companies to send out renewal notices and collect premiums, whilst solicitors might be effectively acting as agent for the insurance company, they are still the client's solicitor and therefore rule 10 applies.

21. What if the insurance company sends me one cheque in respect of various clients and I cannot attribute the commission to individual clients?

In *Brown* v. *I.R.C.* [1965] A.C. 244 Lord Reid said, 'I do not see how the difficulty in discovering who is the owner can make the money the property of the solicitor.' Either make a reasonable estimate as to how much is attributable to each individual client or decline to accept the commission.

22. If I am the sole executor of a will can I consent to myself retaining any commission earned in dealing with the estate?

No. A trustee cannot profit from the trust and rule 10 does not permit a solicitor to retain a commission where this would not be permitted at law. Therefore any commission earned in dealing with the estate should be accounted for to the estate. The same principle would apply to a solicitor who was the donee of a power of attorney.

March 1992, updated December 1995

APPENDIX G
Guidance on ownership, storage and destruction of documents

1. Is the client entitled to the whole file once the retainer is terminated?

Not necessarily. Most files will contain some documents which belong to you, some which belong to the client and possibly others belonging to a third party. Documents in existence before the retainer, held by you as agent for and on behalf of the client or a third party, must be dealt with in accordance with the instructions of the client or third party (subject to your lien). Documents coming into existence during the retainer fall into four broad categories (see also *Cordery on Solicitors*):

(a) **Documents prepared by you for the benefit of the client and which have been paid for by the client, either directly or indirectly, belong to the client.**

Examples: instructions and briefs; most attendance notes; drafts; copies made for the client's benefit of letters received by you; copies of letters written by you to third parties if contained in the client's case file and used for the purpose of the client's business. There would appear to be a distinction between copies of letters written to the client (which may be retained by you) and copies of letters written to third parties.

(b) **Documents prepared by you for your own benefit or protection, the preparation of which is not regarded as an item chargeable against the client, belong to you.**

Examples: copies of letters written to the client; copies made for your own benefit of letters received by you; copies of letters written by you to third parties if contained only in a filing system of all letters written in your office; tape recordings of conversations; inter-office memoranda; entries in diaries; time sheets; computerised records; office journals; books of account.

(c) **Documents sent to you by the client during the retainer, the property in which was intended at the date of despatch to pass from the client to you, belong to you.**

Examples: letters, authorities and instructions written or given to you by the client.

(d) **Documents prepared by a third party during the course of the retainer and sent to you (other than at your expense) belong to the client.**

Examples: receipts and vouchers for disbursements made by you on behalf of the client; medical and witness reports; counsel's advice and opinion; letters received by you from third parties.

2. Who owns the file where there has been a joint retainer?

In the Society's opinion the documents which fall into category (a) above belong to both or all of the clients jointly. Such documents can only be disclosed to third parties with the consent of both or all of the clients and the original papers can only be given to one client with the authority of the other(s). Each client is entitled to a copy of the relevant documents at their own expense. (See also 16.01 note 5, in *The Guide to the Professional Conduct of Solicitors 1996* (the Guide).)

3. Who owns the file where there is a single file but two separate retainers?

This is usually the case where you have acted for the buyer/borrower and for the lender on a contemporaneous purchase and mortgage, or for the borrower and for the new lender on a re-mortgage. You will need to sort through the file to determine the ownership of the various papers (see 1 above). There may, however, be documents which belong to the borrower but which the lender is nevertheless entitled to see as they relate to that part of your work where the lender and borrower can be said to have a common interest, such as the deduction of title, the acquisition of a good title to the property and ancillary legal issues such as the use of the property.

4. How long should I retain old files?

The Society cannot specify how long individual files should be retained. It may be advisable to retain all files for a minimum of six years from when the subject matter was wholly completed. At the end of the six-year period, you should review the files again according to the nature of the particular transactions, and the likelihood of any claims arising. In cases where a party was under a disability at the time of the action or where judgement for provisional damages has been obtained, files should be retained for a minimum period of six years from the date on which the client would have a cause of action, or final judgement has been obtained.

The relevant statutory provisions should also be taken into account and some examples are given:

(a) Under Schedule 7, paragraph 7(2) of the Value Added Tax Act 1983, records and papers relevant to VAT liability have to be kept for six years; this obligation could cover all the papers in a solicitor's file and, subject to Customs and Excise agreeing the contrary in any particular case, the whole file should therefore be kept for this period. This obligation may be discharged by keeping the papers on microfilm or microfiche, but Customs and Excise's detailed requirements should first be checked with the local VAT office.

(b) Section 14A of the Limitation Act 1980 provides a special time limit for negligence actions where facts relevant to the cause of action are not known at the date of accrual. It prevents the bringing of such actions after six years from the date on which the cause of action accrued or three years from the date on which the plaintiff knew or ought to have known the facts, whichever is later. Section 14B provides an overriding time limit of 15 years from the defendant's breach of duty.

5. Can I destroy documents once I have held them for the relevant period?

Before deciding to destroy a file it is essential to consider who owns which documents (see question 1 above). No documents should be destroyed without the prior consent of the owner (but see question 6 below in respect of microfilming). You may always invite clients to take possession of their own papers, balancing the potential saving of space and expense against a possible loss of goodwill.

6. Can I microfilm documents and destroy the originals?

Original documents, such as deeds, guarantees or certificates, which are not your own property, should not be destroyed without the express written permission of the owner. Where the work has been completed and the bill paid, other documents

APPENDIX G: GUIDANCE ON OWNERSHIP, STORAGE AND DESTRUCTION

including your file, may be microfilmed and then destroyed after a reasonable time. In cases of doubt the owner's written permission should always be sought. If it is not possible to obtain such permission you will have to form a view and evaluate the risk. When seeking owners' permission to microfilm and destroy documents, you may wish to reserve the right to make a reasonable charge for preparing copies if they are later requested. See 4(a) above for the requirements of Customs and Excise.

7. What is the evidential value of a microfilm of a document where the original has been destroyed?

There is a dearth of judicial authority on this topic and, until the law and practice on the subject of microfilming are clarified, it is only possible to provide general guidelines. The Society has been advised that:

(a) A microfilm of any document in a solicitor's file will be admissible evidence to the same extent, no more and no less, as the document itself, *provided that* there is admissible evidence of the destruction of the document and identification of the copy.

(b) Written evidence of the destruction of the original and of identification of the copy will enable the microfilm to be adduced in subsequent civil proceedings (under the Civil Evidence Act 1968) and in criminal proceedings (under the Police and Criminal Evidence Act 1984).

8. What procedures would the Society recommend where original documents are microfilmed and then destroyed?

(a) Written evidence of the destruction of the original and of identification of the copy must always be preserved in case oral evidence is no longer available when needed (see 7(b) above).

(b) There should be a proper system for:

    (i) identifying each file or document destroyed;

    (ii) recording that the complete file or document, as the case may be, has been photographed;

    (iii) recording identification by the camera operator of the negatives as copies of the documents photographed; and

    (iv) preserving and indexing the negatives.

(c) If a microfilm record is required to be produced in evidence, a partner or senior member of staff should be able to certify that:

    (i) the document has been destroyed;

    (ii) the microfilm is a true record of that document; and

    (iii) the enlargement is an enlargement of that microfilm recording.

(d) Microfilm copies of some documents (e.g. coloured plans) can be unsatisfactory, in which case the originals should be preserved.

9. Will I be covered by the Solicitors' Indemnity Fund if I lose a client's file or destroy it without the client's consent?

If you incur liability either to a client or to a third party by the loss or destruction of documents, cover will normally be provided by the Solicitors' Indemnity Fund.

10. What happens if I lose a file relating to a claim against my firm?

If the handling or settlement of a claim has been substantially prejudiced by non-compliance with any provision of the Indemnity Rules, Solicitors Indemnity Fund Limited (SIF) is entitled to recover from the firm (or from you personally) the difference between the sum payable by the Fund in respect of the claim and the sum that would have been payable but for the non-compliance – see rule 19.11 of the Indemnity Rules (Annex 29A in the Guide). This could happen if documents were destroyed after a claim had been made or after the firm had knowledge of circumstances likely to give rise to a claim. In such a case, the firm would be in breach of its obligation to allow SIF to take over and to conduct the defence or settlement of the claim. Extra care should, therefore, be taken of any papers that relate to a claim or possible claim.

11. Would the client have grounds for making a complaint if I lost a file, or destroyed it without the client's consent?

The view of the Standards and Guidance Committee is that the storing of deeds and other legal documents for clients is a professional service. The loss or destruction of such documents could, therefore, give rise to an investigation by the Solicitors Complaints Bureau on the basis of inadequate professional services.

APPENDIX G: GUIDANCE ON OWNERSHIP, STORAGE AND DESTRUCTION

12. What if I am holding documents which may be of historical or archival value?

Contact the county archivist to arrange a confidential inspection of the documents. If it is necessary to preserve the confidentiality of archival material due, for example, to the true ownership being in doubt, arrangements should be made with the county archivist for it to be deposited on that basis, so that if the ownership is later established, it can be returned. For further details contact the British Records Association, Records Preservation Section, at 18 Padbury Court, London E2 7EH (0171-729 1415).

13. How can I ensure client confidentiality when destroying old files?

The best way to ensure this is to arrange for the old files to be shredded in the office sufficiently finely to avoid any risk. If that is not possible, while this responsibility remains with the solicitor, it should be possible to contract either with the local council or a member firm of the British Waste Paper Association for their confidential destruction in sealed bags. The Association's address is Alexander House, Station Road, Aldershot, Hants. GU11 1BQ (01252 344454).

December 1986, revised December 1995

APPENDIX H
'Blue card' warning on money laundering – practice information

Could you be involved?

Could you or your firm be unwittingly assisting in the laundering of proceeds of crime? The Criminal Justice Act 1993 (see Annex 16C in *The Guide to the Professional Conduct of Solicitors 1996* (the Guide)) and the Money Laundering Regulations 1993 (Annex 3B in the Guide) mark an important step in the fight against serious crime, in particular against the drugs trade. All solicitors should be aware of the money laundering provisions in the Criminal Justice Act 1993. ***Additionally***, solicitors who engage in investment business within the meaning of the Financial Services Act 1986 are subject to the Money Laundering Regulations 1993, and must take the steps required by the Regulations to ensure that they and their firms cannot be used by money launderers.

Might YOU commit a criminal offence?

If solicitors do not take steps to learn about the provisions of the Criminal Justice Act 1993, they may commit criminal offences, by assisting someone known or suspected to be laundering money generated by any serious crime, by telling clients or anyone else that they are under investigation for an offence of money laundering, or by failing to report a suspicion of money laundering in the case of drug trafficking or terrorism, unless certain exceptions apply. ***Additionally***, solicitors who engage in investment business within the meaning of the Financial Services Act 1986 will commit criminal offences unless they take the steps required by theMoney Laundering Regulations 1993. The Regulations may also apply in certain other circumstances – see 3.16 in the Guide.

As well as the Money Laundering Regulations 1993, the law relating to money laundering in England and Wales is contained in several different Acts:

- the Drug Trafficking Offences Act 1986
- the Criminal Justice Act 1988

APPENDIX H: 'BLUE CARD' WARNING ON MONEY LAUNDERING

- the Prevention of Terrorism (Temporary Provisions) Act 1989
- the Criminal Justice (International Co-operation) Act 1990
- the Drug Trafficking Act 1994

The Criminal Justice Act 1993 amended parts of these Acts.

Guidance on these Acts and their effect on solicitors can be found in 16.07 and Annex 16C in the Guide. *Remember* the Criminal Justice Act 1993 in some cases affected the client's right to confidentiality.

Could you spot a money laundering transaction?

The signs to watch for:

1. **UNUSUAL SETTLEMENT REQUESTS** – Settlement by cash of any large transaction involving the purchase of property or other investment should give rise to caution. Payment by way of third party cheque or money transfer where there is a variation between the account holder, the signatory and a prospective investor should give rise to additional enquiries.

2. **UNUSUAL INSTRUCTIONS** – Care should always be taken when dealing with a client who has no discernible reason for using the firm's services, e.g. clients with distant addresses who could find the same service nearer their home base; or clients whose requirements do not fit into the normal pattern of the firm's business and could be more easily serviced elsewhere.

3. **LARGE SUMS OF CASH** – Always be cautious when requested to hold large sums of cash in your client account, either pending further instructions from the client or for no other purpose than for onward transmission to a third party.

4. **THE SECRETIVE CLIENT** – A personal client who is reluctant to provide details of his or her identity. Be particularly cautious about the client you do not meet in person.

5. **SUSPECT TERRITORY** – Caution should be exercised whenever a client is introduced by an overseas bank, other investor or third party based in countries where production of drugs or drug trafficking may be prevalent.

Investment business – what the law says you must do

Solicitors who engage in investment business within the meaning of the Financial Services Act 1986 must comply with the provisions of the Money Laundering Regulations 1993 (Annex 3B in the Guide). Every firm should keep a copy of the Regulations. In particular, every firm affected by the regulations must:

1. Ensure that all staff who handle investment business are given training in the recognition and handling of suspicious transactions. Every firm must ensure that employees are aware of the firm's policies and procedures for preventing money laundering.

2. Appoint an individual to whom staff can report suspicions of money laundering, and who will be responsible for making a decision on reporting the suspicions to the appropriate authorities.

3. Ensure that they have in place a recognised procedure for obtaining satisfactory evidence of the identity of those with whom they do business, and that records of that evidence of identity are established and kept in respect of each transaction for five years. There are exceptions set out in regulation 10.

4. Establish and maintain for at least five years from the date of the completion of the transaction, a record of each transaction undertaken.

5. Report knowledge or suspicions to the Financial Unit, National Criminal Intelligence Service (see below).

Useful addresses

Disclosure to a constable under the money laundering legislation may be made to the Financial Unit, National Criminal Intelligence Service, Spring Gardens, Vauxhall, London SE11 5EN. Telephone 0171-238 8271 (outside office hours 0171- 238 8607), fax 0171 238 8286.

Further advice and guidance can be obtained from:

The Professional Adviser, Professional and Legal Policy Directorate, The Law Society, 50 Chancery Lane, London WC2A 1SX. Telephone 0171-320 5712; fax 0171-320 5918.

APPENDIX H: 'BLUE CARD' WARNING ON MONEY LAUNDERING

The Joint Money Laundering Steering Group, Information Transfer Limited, Burleigh House, 15 New Market Road, Cambridge CB5 8EG. Telephone 01223-312227; fax 01223-327017.

April 1994, revised December 1995

APPENDIX I
'Green card' warning on property fraud – practice information

Could you be involved or implicated?

Could you be unwittingly assisting in a fraud? The general assumption is that if there has been a property fraud a solicitor *must* have been involved. Solicitors should therefore be vigilant to protect both their clients and themselves. Steps can be taken to minimise the risk of being involved or implicated in a fraud (see below).

Could you spot a property fraud?

The signs to watch for include the following (but this list is not exhaustive):

- **Fraudulent buyer or fictitious solicitors** – especially if the buyer is introduced to your practice by a third party (for example a broker or estate agent) who is not well known to you. Beware of clients whom you never meet and solicitors not known to you.

- **Unusual instructions** – for example a solicitor being instructed by the seller to remit the net proceeds of sale to anyone other than the seller.

- **Misrepresentation of the purchase price** – ensure that the true cash price actually to be paid is stated as the consideration in the contract and transfer and is identical to the price shown in the mortgage instructions and in the report on title to the lender.

- **A deposit or any part of purchase price paid direct** – a deposit or the difference between the mortgage advance and the price, paid direct, or said to be paid direct, to the seller.

- **Incomplete contract documentation** – contract documents not fully completed by the seller's representative, i.e. dates missing or the identity of the parties not fully described or financial details not fully stated.

APPENDIX I: 'GREEN CARD' WARNING ON PROPERTY FRAUD

- **Changes in the purchase price** – adjustments to the purchase price, particularly in high percentage mortgage cases, or allowances off the purchase price, for example, for works to be carried out.

- **Unusual transactions** – transactions which do not follow their normal course or the usual pattern of events:

    (a) client with current mortgage on two or more properties

    (b) client using alias

    (c) client buying several properties from same person or two or more persons using same solicitor

    (d) client reselling property at a substantial profit, for which no explanation has been provided.

What steps can I take to minimise the risk of fraud?

Be vigilant: if you have any doubts about a transaction, consider whether any of the following steps could be taken to minimise the risk of fraud:

- **Verify the identity and bona fides of your client and solicitors' firms you do not know** – meet the clients where possible and get to know them a little. Check that the solicitor's firm and office address appear in the *Directory of Solicitors and Barristers* or contact the Law Society's Records Centre (PSD) (Tel: 0171–242 1222).

- **Question unusual instructions** – if you receive unusual instructions from your client discuss them with your client fully.

- **Discuss with your client any aspects of the transaction which worry you** – if, for example, you have any suspicion that your client may have submitted a false mortgage application or references, or if the lender's valuation exceeds the actual price paid, discuss this with your client. If you believe that the client intends to proceed with a fraudulent application, you must refuse to continue to act for the buyer and the lender.

- **Check that the true price is shown in all documentation** – check that the actual price paid is stated in the contract, transfer and mortgage instructions. Where you are also acting for a lender, tell your client that you will have to cease acting unless the client permits you to report to the lender all allowances and incentives. See also the guidance printed in [1990] *Gazette*, 12 December, 16 [see Annex 25F in *The Guide to the Professional Conduct of Solicitors 1996*].

COMPLYING WITH THE SOLICITORS' ACCOUNTS RULES: A PRACTICAL GUIDE

- **Do not witness pre-signed documentation** – no document should be witnessed by a solicitor or his or her staff unless the person signing does so in the presence of the witness. If the document is pre-signed, ensure that it is re-signed in the presence of a witness.

- **Verify signatures** – consider whether signatures on all documents connected with a transaction should be examined and compared with signatures on any other available documentation.

- **Make a company search** – where a private company is the seller, or the seller has purchased from a private company in the recent past, and you suspect that the sale may not be on proper arm's length terms, you should make a search in the Companies Register to ascertain the names and addresses of the officers and shareholders, which can then be compared with the names of those connected with the transaction and the seller and buyer.

Remember that, even where investigations result in a solicitor ceasing to act for a client, the solicitor will still owe a duty of confidentiality which would prevent the solicitor passing on information to the lender. It is only where the solicitor is satisfied that there is a strong *prima facie* case that the client was using the solicitor to further a fraud or other criminal purpose that the duty of confidentiality would not apply.

Any failure to observe these signs and to take the appropriate steps may be used in court as evidence against you if you and your client are prosecuted, or if you are sued for negligence.

Further guidance can be obtained from the Law Society's Practice Advice Service (Tel: 0171–242 1222).

March 1991, revised January 1996

APPENDIX J
Warning issued by the Law Society regarding "scams"

The ingenuity of fraudsters makes it impossible to define and list all indicators of financial/investment scams, but here are some factors which the Society has come across. Remember that all cons are plausible!

Firms at greatest risk

- Fraudsters need to use solicitors' firms to give authenticity to a scam or to advise a client who is the real victim. They will often choose small firms or sole practitioners, perhaps operating in a main financial centre such as London.

Advance fees for loans

- A typical target is a client who needs a loan but is unable to raise one through normal sources. Before the promised loan is paid (often a large sum at a reasonable rate of interest), your client will have to make a payment (variously referred to as a "processing fee", "arrangement fee" or "commission") or will be asked to pay for "expenses", such as air tickets or hotel bills. Sometimes a larger "returnable" advance is required from the client in order to secure a larger loan. These advances may be made on security of an undertaking from another firm of solicitors who may themselves have been the subject of a con. The loan never materialises.

- The loan is often stated to be a small part of a much larger lending ability, e.g. if a client wishes to borrow £1 million, it would be typical for the fraudster to say that the fictitious lenders had £2 billion at their disposal.

- The borrower will never meet the lender because the lender doesn't exist. A good way of uncovering one of these frauds is to press the fraudster for detailed information about the lender.

Money for nothing

- The deal will often promise a generous fee to the firm for apparently little work.

Meaningless jargon

- The supporting paperwork will be full of complex financial jargon, e.g. "self-liquidating loan scheme"; "prime bank notes, mature and fresh cut". You may be asked to be a "secure third party independent account holder for good clean funds for immediate payment against authenticated collateral" (translation: "Please issue a client account cheque now; you will (?) get the money later.") While you may assume that these terms mean something to City firms, it may not be so. Often the terminology is pure gobbledegook – but the solicitors targeted may be too proud, or influenced by the promised fee, to admit a lack of understanding.

False claims to reputable bankers

- There will frequently be general references to backing by top world/British banks, foreign governments or reputable international organisations, such as the United Nations. If you are unsure, check with the organisations who are said to be involved. Check that any banks you haven't heard of really exist.

Requests for details of client account

- Beware of complex schemes which, on the surface, are requests to send large amounts of money to you for safe-keeping. If you are required to send details of your bank, client account numbers, blank stationery and any letter with your signature, beware. Such information and documents can be used to make unauthorised withdrawals from your client account!

Sales of shares

- If you have custody of a client's share certificates, ensure that they are kept in a secure place (e.g. a safe) and not merely left in the file. There have been cases of certificates being stolen and the fraudster using a solicitor to arrange for their sale. If you are asked to act in this way and you don't know the client check his or her identity and *bona fides*.

APPENDIX J: WARNING ISSUED BY THE LAW SOCIETY REGARDING "SCAMS"

In short, don't give any form of undertaking to guarantee a financial obligation unless you have funds or equivalent security. The word of someone "backed by a major international bank" is not enough. If asked to provide money from client account on the security of another firm's undertaking, ask that firm for evidence of their ability to comply. Never send a client account cheque on the basis of a verbal confirmation that the money is on its way into your client account – check it's there.

Some of these situations can be awkward as, often, the client will be pressing you to take part in what appears to be an offer that is too good to be true – which it probably is!

If you have come across these sophisticated scams, please pass on the information to the Society. The Compensation and Indemnity Funds both have an interest – as do your professional colleagues.

May 1993